You're Not Crazy You Have A Ghost

"You're Not Crazy: You Have A Ghost"

Revised Edition

Rick L. Hayes & K. Coons

Stellium Books
Grant Park Illinois 60940

You're Not Crazy You Have A Ghost

Stellium Books

Copyright 2004 2015 by Rick L. Hayes

All rights reserved. Published in the United States .

All rights reserved. Any reproduction of the book without the express written consent is prohibited. The authors of this book assume no responsibility for the actions of those other than the authors themselves.

Cover Design by Annette Munnich

Manufactured in the United States of America

Revised Edition: 2015
ISBN 9780692594155

Table Of Contents

Introduction – The Unsuspecting New Home Owner
Introduction – "Rick's Thoughts" v vii

Chapter I: I Bought A Home With Secrets	1
Chapter II: The Beginning Of Visual Contact	15
Chapter III: Restoration With Unseen Assistance	27
Chapter IV: A Background Check On Reality	43
Chapter V: Mommy, I Am Scared!	55
Chapter VI: The Face In The Steam	71
Chapter VII: Family Togetherness	85
Chapter VIII: A Call To The PI	95
Chapter IX: Lessons of Understanding	107
Chapter X: Now Let Us Review	121
Chapter XI: A Final Word	131
Bonus Chapter I A Nursery for our New Arrival	137
Bonus Chapter II Knocks and Screams	145
Bonus Chapter III New Friendships	151
Bonus Chapter IV Life After the Home	155
Photos	161
About the Authors	164

Introduction

The Unsuspecting New Home Owner

You purchase your dream home and nothing seems right. As soon as you move into your new place things seem to be happening that you cannot explain. Are you just tired and stressed from the move? Maybe you are just uncomfortable being in a new place. You convince yourself that in a few days you will settle down and everything will be "normal" again.

You may have purchased this book because things did not go back to "normal" as you knew it before. Things that seem to be impossible keep on happening. Have you gone crazy? Do you have a ghost? I am one of those unsuspecting homebuyers and I want to share with you experiences my family has endured in the past five years. My friend and co-writer also experiences things but through his abilities as a medium. The book is a workbook for people just like me that have purchased a home or piece of real estate, and is experiencing the paranormal. In the following pages we will share with you my own personal experiences; in hopes with this workbook we can help you to feel comfortable with the unexplained. My family can relate to yours; ready to sell the house and run away. I looked for books that would calm my nerves, but found only publications that terrified me even more.

You're Not Crazy You Have A Ghost

I know from my own personal experience that if a workbook had been available, it would have helped me to stay a lot calmer during the first few years. I hope that we can help you get through what you are experiencing in your life. I will share with you some of my experiences, followed by my friend's commentary on what is going on from a "mediums" point of view. Please use this workbook and learn to live with your experiences in a different perspective. I believe when you complete the workbook, you will end up just like my family did...You wouldn't trade this experience for anything and selling your home is now completely out of the question!

Introduction

Rick's Thoughts

Shadows appear around the corner. Whispers from the unknown are echoing in the upstairs of your home. Sounds of unseen footsteps climb up and down the stairway. All the while you keep asking yourself "Is it my imagination or am I going crazy?"

You have purchased this workbook for one of two reasons: Your curiosity set in when you read the title, or you are living in a home that reflects the first paragraph. "You're Not Crazy, You Have a Ghost" is written to share with you the understanding that you are not alone. Many are curious in regards to life-after death, and strive to find answers.

The topic of paranormal experiences, spiritual enlightenment, and life everlasting is becoming more and more popular in today's society. You may even know of a house or building that is so-called "haunted", or possibly living in one right now while trying to determine if it is real or imagination. We especially wrote this book for you. We want to share with you the fact that many others are experiencing in their own residences what you are, including the co-writer of this workbook. "You're Not Crazy, You Have A Ghost" is a work-book created to give you step-by-step guidelines on what to expect, how to cope, and to bring comfort to you and your "visitors". At the end of each section, you will find a "Notes" section designed to write down your own experiences and thoughts.   You will also read "personal experiences"

from the co-writer, as well as a "follow-up thought" from a medium's point of view.

   Let's get started by moving on to the first section, and by the end of this workbook you will feel comfort, hope, faith, and above all know that "You're Not Crazy".

You're Not Crazy You Have A Ghost

My Notes

Before I begin to read this book, my personal experiences are:

You're Not Crazy You Have A Ghost

Before I begin to read this book, my personal experiences are (cont.):

You're Not Crazy You Have A Ghost

Before I begin to read this book, my personal experiences are (cont.):

Before I begin to read this book, my personal experiences are (cont.):

You're Not Crazy You Have A Ghost

Before I begin to read this book, my personal experiences are (cont.):

Chapter I

I Bought A Home With Secrets

When I found my 1906 Queen Anne home in mid-western America it was a total wreck. I had always loved antiques and wanted to restore an old home. This was also a time in my life when I felt like I had nothing to lose. I had just ended a very nasty divorce and had lost everything I owned. I was finally getting my act together and met a great guy, who later became my husband. Between the two of us we have six kids and two dogs. We were looking for space that an older home provided. We found such a home and the price was right. My husband and I were convinced that the home would be a lot of cosmetic work, boy were we wrong! I was working at the time for a real estate firm when our dream home appeared on the market. I just felt this was the home we were looking for, and anxiously wanted to see it right away. My boss kept discouraging me on purchasing the home. He kept telling me that I didn't know what I was getting in to, and old houses are always more work than they appear. My boss realized that he wasn't going to change my mind about the house, so he insisted that I have the home inspected.

He set the appointment with a home inspector that he recommended very highly. Upon final analysis, the home inspector let us know the foundation of the home was in great shape. The home's previous owners before our purchase included a temporary nurse assistance business. Since the home was a business, it had been updated with new electrical, new furnaces and new windows. This just seemed too good to be true... this should have been my first clue. We investigated our home many times before we decided to purchase; each time with a feeling like someone was watching me. I even remember walking into where my daughters room is and saying "I know you are here". I convinced myself that it was an old house and my imagination was going wild. The day finally came to sign the papers on our new home. When I arrived at the bank for the closing, the lady I was buying the house from seemed very nervous. She couldn't get the papers signed fast enough and even made the statement, "Congratulations better you than me". By this time I am extremely nervous. I thought to myself "oh great I have made the biggest mistake of my life". I kept wondering what it was that I would find wrong with the house?

   I took my mother and a few of my close friends on a tour of my soon- to-be dream home. They thought I had lost my mind! I had bought a dump without hope was the comments that I received. I convinced them (and myself) that it would be beautiful when completed. My mom, while still not convinced, said she got the strangest feeling when she went upstairs to our family room area. She said in the room she had a very strange sense of calm that she had never felt before.

Two weeks later, my daughter had four of her girlfriends to stop by. We were having our annual town Fall Fest and the girls wanted to see our new home. The girls took the typical house tour and ended up in the family room upstairs. All the girls were sitting around waiting for each one to return from the rest room. I was also at the time upstairs, and could hear the girl's conversation. One of the girls stated, "I feel weird. I am so calm. Can we just stay here"? Another girl replied "yea me too". I was really freaked out by all of this, as it was exactly what my mother had said a few weeks earlier. I thought it was strange also that a bunch of 12 year old girls would rather sit in my family room with the TV off than go back to the festival just down the street where all their other friends were. During the week of the festival we received many visitors. The parade route went right in front of our house, so a lot of our friends were going to sit in our yard and watch it. Everyone came to our house early with his or her kids. We gave the new house tours while the kids played in our family room. It was now time for the parade to start, so we anxiously gathered our kids together so as to get everyone organized in the front yard. I was the last one out of the house and realized that the kids had left television on upstairs. I went upstairs to turn the television off. I turned the television off and started down our back stairs when half the way down I heard the television come back on. I thought we had forgotten one of the kids and went back up to search for them. I could not locate anyone as everyone was on the front lawn waiting for the parade. I turned the television off.

Again it came right back on. I decided to leave the television on and join the rest of my guests on the front lawn and believe me I joined them in quick fashion. This would be only the beginning of the problems we would experience with our electrical appliances. I was beginning to suspect things were not "normal" in my house. I was too scared to sleep with the lights out and always kept my television on in my room. The next thing I knew, the television began going on and off during the night. My kids also refused to sleep without having lights or the television on. They were also experiencing the lights and the television being turned on and off in the middle of the night. CD players would change songs without assistance; lights would flicker and sometimes even go out with no explanation, alarm clocks would ring at all times. Then we started hearing footsteps on the front
stairs, and the sounds of the cabinet doors in the kitchen were being open and closed in the middle of the night. By this time, everyone in my family was getting nervous and we didn't know what to think or do. We didn't know if we should talk about this or just keep it to ourselves. Everyone would think we had lost our minds.

    My husband accepted a position at his place of employment where he worked nights. This didn't help, as strange things seemed to be happening even more frequently. I finally told my Mother what was going on. I was a little afraid to bring up something so weird to anyone in my family. We were raised as very strict Christians and this goes against everything I had been taught as a child. My mom said she would spend the night at my house and see what I was experiencing. We agreed that it would be good if she slept in my room for the night and that she would place the TV remote in a different place. She would place it somewhere that I would not know to see what might happen. I was beginning to think maybe the change in address and the stress of my new life was getting to me. But if I was crazy, everyone else in my home was losing it too. We turned in for the night hoping for a night of restful sleep. At 3:00 am it happened, the television went off in my room. This time, my mother was present to be my witness. When we both looked toward the television we could see a blue misty light around that area. My mom turned on the light quickly and hurried to pick up the remote where she had hid it. The remote was placed exactly as she had left it. Both of us were really frightened, and my mother didn't know what to think. I begin to explain to her that events like this take place all the time in this house. Now I was really questioning if we should sell the house to another unsuspecting homebuyer or not. Now all the logical explanations for what was going on seemed to be diminishing as quickly as I had hoped for.

If you are experiencing anything similar to what my family went through, please use the workbook provided at the end of this chapter to document what is going on. I know you feel like you are going crazy right now but be patient, things will soon become clearer.

Rick's Thoughts

By now you have finished this chapter with one of two opinions in your mind. The question is which opinion do you have? If you have experienced similar situations as the fact-based accounts above, you are nodding your head and already skipping to the "Notes" section to write down your own personal experiences. The other option is that you are shaking your head wondering if this actually occurred, as it is not in the common scientific belief that it is possible at all.

A house when built is just that, a house. When you move into a house, you begin to build the memories and create the love within the house. These tools turn the house into a home. Think about the first time you moved into your home. Remember the unpacking of boxes and the moving of furniture? The smell of fresh paint as you brought your own personal colors upon the interior walls. Now think about the first night you stayed in your home. The excitement and accomplishment still in your heart, and the thrill of waking up and watching the sun rise through you bedroom window. Add the many years of memories in the home. The holiday festivities and the many nights the family sat together just to talk. The sharing of sadness and the happiness of love that are experienced. So many memories turn a house into a home. The home is a place of security. You may be setting in your favorite chair right now while reading this book. Do you not feel safe because you are home?

It is my personal belief that when one's earthly body is done on earth, the spirit moves-on to live forever. I believe this because our creator loves us.

The spirit of a loved-one is with us to assist in our earthly plan. Sometimes, I feel that a spirit will also help those they did not know while on earth, but may have taken residence in the house that the spirit transformed with love into a home. It is my opinion they mean no harm to you, but rather utilize ways for you to seek their attention.

Remember when your child wanted your attention, and you were very busy at the time and unintentionally ignored the child? What did the child do? Did the child walk away, or did the child use some type of physical attraction such as raising their voice or possibly even grabbing you by the arm? The child may have even tried to grab an object or threw an object on the floor. So, did they receive your attention at that time? I believe your answer will be a common one.

I feel this is the same for spirits (or ghosts) in your home. They want you to understand of their presence, and sometimes that may utilize some type of physical contact. By slamming doors, moving objects or by creating a feeling of a presence, they attract your attention. The next thing you should do, as with a child, is to find out the reason why. I believe that they have a message for you when these things occur. Is it to merely frighten you into moving out? Most probably not, but by listening and understanding you may soon find your answer. Opinion one or opinion two? One thing is for sure, the next chapter is a must read for either opinion.

You're Not Crazy You Have A Ghost

My notes as I read:

You're Not Crazy You Have A Ghost

My notes as I read:

You're Not Crazy You Have A Ghost

My notes as I read:

You're Not Crazy You Have A Ghost

My notes as I read:

You're Not Crazy You Have A Ghost

My notes as I read:

You're Not Crazy You Have A Ghost

My notes as I read:

Chapter II

The Beginning of Visual Contact

As I mentioned earlier logical explanations for my houses strange occurrences diminished fast. If you are having similar experiences in your house read on and see if the next set of things are happening to you also. The first incident I had with actually seeing anything was when the TV went off in my bedroom and I thought I saw a blue light around where the TV was. I rationalized this and thought it must be something to do with electricity or the TV. I didn't give the blue light glow I had seen too much thought until it seemed like I was catching more glimpses of this. I usually see this around a light or an electrical appliance. I still do not know for sure what it is, but I do know this happens often. Most of the time when I see this, the room seems very electrically charged. This never really scared me too much. I see this so fast I am usually not even sure if it is real or not. But if you have a house like mine it probably is real. I am still looking for an explanation for this. All I know is that I never had this happen in any other homes I lived in. We occasionally experience mists or fogs in our house. I remember one time I was upstairs and decided to go downstairs by way of my back staircase. This staircase leads directly into my kitchen. When I reached the bottom of the stairs and was standing in the kitchen I noticed a mist or fog around the entire ceiling of my kitchen. My first reaction was this was smoke. I ran to the stove thinking something had been left in the oven and was burning. Nothing was in the oven or on the stove, as we had not been cooking. I wondered why none of the smoke detectors had worked. I also noticed that I didn't smell any smoke either. I just stood there in my kitchen watching this fog like mist; it seemed to be swirling at times like a fan or something was making it move. There is a not fan in my kitchen and no windows were open. Soon the fog disappeared and all at once. The occurrence that I experience the most is what my family now calls walking through the ghosts. To best explain this is you can be just going about your regular routine cleaning or just walking around the house. As you are walking around you cannot see anything strange but just out of the corner of your eye you will catch a mist or shadow figure. It is like you have just walked through something or walked by someone. Sometimes it appears only as a gray mist and other times you will actually catch a glimpse of a shadow or even a person standing in an area. Everyone in my house has been experiencing this. At first it scared us, we didn't know what we were seeing. My kids seen this very often and would just take off running out of the room. If you have something like this going on please use the workbook to document where you see this and at what times in the day. Also document who seems to be experiencing this most often in your family.

   This will later help to calm your nerves and even to help identify your entity. We have become comfortable with our haunted house, now when we experience this we just say hi or excuse me I didn't see you there. It seems to humor our unseen friends. The experiences seem to most happen when you are relaxed and not focusing on anything special.

We do see floating lights or orbs as my kids call them. These have even showed up in many pictures we have taken in our house. The time the most showed up was at our annual Halloween Party. If you own a Haunted House you have the town's annual Halloween Party. When we had our pictures developed there were orbs everywhere in the pictures. In my home we see these orbs around my front staircase the most. As you start down the front stairs you just might catch a glimpse of a floating ball of light. Once again document where and when you see these.

As I have mentioned many times in this chapter keep good documentation of places, times and who is experiencing these things or similar things the most.

Later this will help you to maybe be able to identify who is sharing your home. It will also help with getting to know your spirit friends personality.

Staircase at the Victorian Photo courtesy of the author

Rick's Thoughts

"I would say you were dreaming". "So what medication have you been taking?" "Do you really expect anyone to believe you?" "It must have been a coincidence." I am sure each one of you has heard these remarks in your life when you tried to explain something that was unnatural to the norm. Society has determined the roles of what is natural and what must be determined as "an imaginative response". At the same time, what was determined fifty years ago as "you must be dreaming" is now concrete reality. Let us look at a few examples:

- In 1943, man landing on the moon was a "dream that will not happen."
- In 1943, cooking with microwave waves meant you had "too much medication or had been drinking."
- In 1943, to have the ability to send messages or capture images by way of a product called a computer was "something that was considered impossible."

We can even go back to biblical times and consider the great words that were written.

How many of those do you think told Moses "you are dreaming" when he said he had spoken to God in a burning bush? How many laughed at Noah when he spent all of those years to build a grand ark, chastising him and with mockery stated "Do you expect us to believe you?"

I have always believed that at birth our minds are created pure of thoughts. We are more astute to our surroundings and with an ability to accept what we feel or see. As we grow older, society "retrains" our minds to only accept what is logical. Remember as a child having an imaginary friend to play games with when you were alone? Today you would be taken to a child psychologist. What about the times you relayed to your parents that there was somebody in your room during the night? Today you would be given prescribed doses of medication. The fact of the matter is that as we grow older and become a part of society's rules of belief and culture, our created pure mind becomes a memory.

Please understand that I do believe that at times we tend to "over imagine" what should be logical, but also at times what is not logical is defined as "over imagined." As I have stated in an earlier chapter, I have had the opportunity to visit the home that is the focal point of this book. I became involved when the mists swirling around in the kitchen and the eerie feeling of someone in the room could not be defined as logical or imagined. Because of my abilities, I do not necessarily need the physical evidence. For example, when I was invited to this home for the very first time I felt the presence of energies upon entering the home. I was in a group of friends invited to tour the home, but also to see if I "felt" anything. I have seen a mist many times since then in the home, along with actual photographs of unexplained images from within the home. Notably most important is that I have been able to assist the homeowner and the energies to understand.

   The key is the ability to understand. A wise man once said: "You have nothing to fear, but fear itself". I will add my own little quote as an addition to this statement.

"You have nothing to fear but fear itself, but to understand will eliminate fear."

   Think about it for a moment. If something frightens you it is the fear of not knowing. Once you understand, you become less frightened. Let's look at an example. In the house that is the focal point of this book, when friends came over to visit they felt a sense of calm. They couldn't explain the reason for the feeling, but never the less it was a feeling that did not frighten them. As the physical attributions began such as the television going off and on, the sense of fear started. The situation did not have a logical meaning. As the homeowner later understood the reasons for the friendly situations, her fear became less apparent. As you continue to read the following chapters, you will also learn more about understanding and less about the emotion of fear.

My notes as I read:

You're Not Crazy You Have A Ghost

My notes as I read:

My notes as I read:

You're Not Crazy You Have A Ghost

My notes as I read:

My notes as I read:

Chapter III

Restoration With Unseen Assistance

If you think the experiences that you have read so far are strange and may even be familiar, read on. The experiences in my new and mysterious home begin to get progressively more intense. I am going to share with you the things that I cannot even begin to believe how my family has learned how to cope with in our new lives.I had made my decision to try and ignore the problems that we were experiencing in the house and move on with the task of restoring this grand old and neglected home. As you entered the house, the gasp would exit from your lips as the existing interior decorum was bathed in baby blue carpet. Highlighting the colorful carpet was the eye-catching wallpaper of hot pink and blue. The disappointment came when we noticed the glorious woodwork had been painted with layers upon layers of paint. As we recovered from the initial shock of bright colors, my husband and I decided to roll up our sleeves and get started on our renovation.

We decided to start with our formal living room. As we were working on the room, both of us continued to feel a presence of some sort. Toward the end of the living room project, we decided to tackle the task of the old fireplace. The very hot summer day brought beads of sweat rolling down our brow, but we continued to take on the task of the fireplace renovation anyway. Finally accomplishing our mission, we opened the fireplace flue. All of a sudden, strong gusts of cold air seem to dissolve the sweat off of our brow. The temperature seemed to immediately drop in the whole room. My husband and I both stood in awe not knowing what to think or do. There was absolutely no reason on a day when the weather outside was sunny, humid and nearly 100 degrees outside could this be possible.

   The installation of the homes central air was still on the "things to do" project list. My husband looked over at me with a very funny stare, and I could not even whisper an answer. The next room to renovate was our dining room. This room had wallpaper that absolutely needed to be stripped and removed. After the grueling task of removing the paper, I remember my husband and I standing in the dining room discussing (in a sort of argument way) how we were going to restore the room. I wanted to select a style of wallpaper that reflected the time period of the house. My husband, who despises the task of wallpapering, kept insisting on painting the dining room. We were getting quite upset with each other and our argument was becoming rather loud. During this time we did not realize that another opinion from a resident of the home would become involved in our final decision. When I would address the reasons for wallpapering, the lights in the room suddenly dimmed. When my husband stated a case for painting, the lights would suddenly become brighter.

This went on for some time, and I finally said with loud and loving compassion "I don't care what you think, we are wallpapering this room". Just as the sentence came from my mouth the lights went completely out in the room. My husband, getting ready to walk out of the room quickly turned around and said, "Why did you do that for?" I was standing there in the middle of the room feeling totally dumb founded. My husband rather upset with me by now and still thinking I had flipped the lights off on him, walked over to the switch on the wall and tried to turn the lights on.

He flipped the switch several times, to no avail. At this time we had not replaced any of the light fixtures and every room was equipped with ceiling fans. You know the kind, the type with five light fixtures on every fan. My husband finally decided to walk over to the pull chains hanging down from the fan light fixture and pull the chain. Just as he pulled the chain, the lights all came back on!

We still cannot explain the reason for the light controls, and we even had an electrician later inspect the lights for us. Upon inspection, the electrician simply could not give to us an explanation. As you might have guessed, our dining room is PAINTED a lovely shade of burgundy. Believe me; I do not think the room will ever be wallpapered again.

I was beginning to get the feeling that whatever the unseen force we had in our house, they wanted us to keep on working on the restoration. In fact, they seemed to have a lot of interest in it. I also felt that whoever they were the energies must have been a previous owner and adored there home with passion. We decided to continue working on the restoration.

The next project on the list was to remove the horrible wheelchair ramp from our front porch. The previous owners had occupied the house as a business and it had been equipped with a wheel chair ramp coming off the side of our soon-to-be lovely porch. The porch had been badly neglected as weeds were growing between the planks of the porch flooring. My husband and his teenage son accomplished ripping the wheelchair ramp from the porch.

They each later acknowledged that as they were working on this removing the ramp, they felt like unseen eyes were watching them. Even when they started to remove the nails from the boards, it was as if someone or something was assisting. Looking back I now feel that whoever was with us simply was applauding our efforts.

One of the reasons we did not move from our home while all of this was happening was simply because of the financial commitment we had already put ourselves into. Take it from a friend; it can produce a mass amount of expenses to restore an old home (added to the fact that both my husband and I had ex-spouses.) As you can guess we not only had the expense of the house but additional expenses of attorney's fees due to our ex-spouses deciding to add to our struggles. Have you ever felt a sense of pride and was not going to let anything or anyone allow you to accept failure? That is exactly how I felt as my pride gave me a renewed direction. I just wasn't going to fail so I learned to defeat whatever was thrown at me.

With each project that we completed, it seemed that our friendly and small town was beginning to take more of an interest. Neighbors around our home and others living in our small community were stopping by and requesting tours. Our home had been many things over the past one hundred years; many of them had been inside the home at one time or another in their lives and were very curious of what we had done. We received some very strange questions from almost everyone who stopped by to visit. For example, questions such as "does the front door stay closed now?" or "do the lights still come on by themselves?" I suspected a lot of the interest in our house came from the fact that they wanted to meet the crazy people who bought the haunted house. I also felt that everyone but my family knew that our house was haunted. We finally met our neighbor next door and in a conversation found out that they had lived in our house when it was an apartment. They wanted to come in and see the changes we had made. After they took the tour, our neighbor asked with a serious expression across his face "do you still have strange things going on over here?" We finally broke down and talked about the occurrences with someone other than within our immediate family. Our neighbor just laughed and said not to worry as the entity in the home is very friendly and will not hurt anyone. This was the first time in months that I felt that maybe I was not going crazy after all. He proceeded to tell us some of the experiences his family had. They had once left on vacation and had a niece enter the house to take care of their pet dog. On the third day she came up to the house and noticed all the lights were on in the house. She was afraid someone may have been in the house and called the local police. When the police arrived, they noticed that all the doors were locked and no evidence of forced entry. They went in to the house to investigate and found nothing out of place or missing.

   A few days later, I met another one of our close neighbors and they asked us if the lights were still coming on by themselves? After talking to them they told us that if it ever happens the local police will not respond to the call. The reason was that while the house was a business before we purchased the house, they would notice the lights going on and off within the home all the time. When they drove by, no vehicles were in the drive and no one within the home. Neighbors would call the business owner on several occasions to let her know what was going on. She would then call the police. The police would arrive each time and investigate. On every occasion the house would be locked and no sign of forced entry. Nothing was out of place and nothing would be missing. Finally the police came up with a theory that the local teen-age kids were climbing up the television antenna tower that was attached to the side of the house and climbing through the window upstairs. This didn't make any sense because the windows were painted shut and nothing was ever found to be out of place. The owner took down the antenna and the lights continued to turn on and off. Finally, the police told the business owner and nearby neighbors not to call back. The neighbors felt that the Police were simply scared of "the haunted house". Once again we were relieved to hear someone else had some very weird things happen to him or her in this old house. My husband also found that one of his co-worker's mother was employed as a nurse at our house when it was a business. She relayed to him that the nurses working in the house would only work together in pairs and never alone. While in the house they would hear the sounds of footsteps climbing up and down the stairs, or shuffling noises in the kitchen while they worked. None of the employed nurses would ever work alone in the house.

I can still recall all of these things like they just happened yesterday. I do wish I had a journal like this one to keep track of how I felt every time something occurred or I found evidence. I still do not like to be in the dark in my home. Not because I am afraid anymore of who or what is here but just because I do not like to be startled. If you live in a haunted house you become startled all the time. Keep track of your feelings when things occur. You will eventually become comfortable in your home and will look back at these very scary, trying times and feel proud that you made it through the experience.

Victorian dining room photos courtesy of the author

Rick's Thoughts

Intuitions, sixth sense, coincidence....I know at one time in your life you have uttered these words to describe an occurrence that you could not explain. At some point in your life you have experienced the "guidance from a loved-one". For example, have you thought about taking a trip and something or someone appeared to be whispering to you to cancel or delay the trip, only to find out later it was the right thing to do? Or have you had the experience of suddenly thinking about someone, and immediately the phone rings and he or she are on the other end? How about waking suddenly in the middle of the night and feel like you should check on something or someone, and to find that it was the right time to do so and preempted what may have happened? I believe that the ones who have moved on have the blessed ability to communicate with those still in their earthly plan (alive on earth). Even more blessed, is that they are given the ability to guide with perfection along with assistance from our creator. Unfortunately, our imperfect abilities while on our life's plan on earth do not allow us to listen. Again we become stubborn in our thoughts, and disregard our guidance as mere coincidence. Let us take a look at a routine scenario that I am sure we can all associate with.

It is a typical early Monday morning for this particular family of five. The husband is scampering about the bathroom trying to make it to his job on time. He had hit the snooze button on the alarm one too many times that morning, and was running late. The wife, also scampering to make it to her job on time, is down in the kitchen trying to find where she had left the cereal bars. Two of the three children are in High School. The young teenage son, with his earphones attached into his ears, grabs a fruit juice out of the refrigerator and heads to school slamming the door as he leaves. The teenage daughter is still upstairs, having a panic attack as her favorite top that she had planned on wearing today is still in the laundry basket. No matter where you would turn in this house on this cloudy Monday morning, you slammed directly into total chaos. Remember I mentioned that there were five in this family? Well among the scamper and stress, setting in his high chair is the cute little one who is all of two years old. While everyone else in his loving family is running to find answers to their own dilemma, he has his own. The little one is strapped safely in his high chair, but his milk bottle is setting just in front of him on the kitchen table. His little voice lets out a small sound hoping to get mom's attention, to no avail. Dad comes running by to grab his cup of coffee. The little one holds out both of his tiny hands, only to see dad fly by in a blur. He tries to reach for the bottle again, only to find that his little arms will not succeed. Finally, he does the one thing that works every time.

    The little one's bright blue eyes well up with tears, and lets out a loud and shrilling scream. It worked, but unfortunately for the little one only for a brief moment.

As his mom runs by to yell at the teenage daughter to hurry up, she puts a small spoon and cereal bowl on the little one's high chair tabletop. He looks down at the bowl and spoon. He begins to wonder why they do not understand that all he wanted was for someone to hand him his bottle. He looks around and screams one more time.

This time everyone completely ignored the high pitched sound coming from the tiny tot. That was it. The little one grabbed the bowl of cereal with his tiny little hands, picked it up, and threw the bowl with all the power his little body could muster. Milk and cereal went flying and found a landing all across the floor and kitchen table. Mom and Dad immediately turned their attention toward their little baby son with startled looks on their faces. Achieving their attention, he again pointed at the bottle. Mom walked toward her son while grabbing a towel from the cabinet, and gave the little one his bottle.

A story to express a point, but the end results is the same. Sometimes when we ignore what we are being told by ones who have moved on they must find other ways to grab our attention. Moving objects, turning lights and appliances on and/or off, creating noises of footsteps and cold air, all of these are simply their way of getting you to pay attention and listen for what they want to relay to you. It is not to frighten you, but rather it is to guide you. In our daily lives we tend to ignore a lot of things about life, but the ones who have moved on completely understand life. Possibly the reason for painting the room instead of wallpapering was simply the energy's way to express that by painting the room it will bring back to the home the ambiance of days past, when he built the home for his own loving family (I use the title He at this point as I later found out who the energy was, and you will too by reading on in this book). He possibly wanted to establish the memories of love created in the home while painting the room, and that arguments between those who love each other are basically a moot point in overall life. There may have been other reasons, but I do know that the energy in the room guides with perfection along with assistance from the creator.

My co-writer's story continues to establish a mysterious intrigue. The more you read on about her experience with her charming home and friendly house guests, you may find yourself in association with her local community at the beginning. They wanted to believe it was all a coincidence. They wanted to believe that it had an earthly and scientific explanation. If you speak with the local community today, they will answer you with "Oh the house that has ghosts'. The community has accepted the fact. My co-writer and family have accepted the fact. Asyou continue to read this book, and learn the steps to accept, you will also accept the fact. Intuition, sixth sense, coincidence… simply communications from ones who have moved on.

My notes as I read:

My notes as I read:

You're Not Crazy You Have A Ghost

My notes as I read:

My notes as I read:

Chapter IV

A Background Check On Reality

I was really beginning to take a renewed and invigorating interest in our home's restoration. For some unexplained reason, I felt that I was being pushed to continue the renovation projects by an unseen force. Even though the somewhat frightening occurrences that was going on and the evidence of the unseen guest taking an interest, I took it upon myself to make sure everything was done right (for obvious reasons).

I decided to try to restore this home as accurately as possible, so I spent many hours researching the history of the home. The first place I went to was our local library. I not only was hoping to find any old pictures of my home, but also gain insight into who our entity was that may have been our "special guest". While researching the library files, I came across a book that had been written for our town's sesquencential celebration. Unfortunately, the book did not include any pictures of my home, but did include a picture of the original owner who had built the house.

I had a feeling inside of me that he may be our home's entity, but was still unsure. After the library research, I spoke to several of our neighbors to find out anything they could recall about how our home may have looked in the past. Most of the ones that I spoke with could only remember how the home's design was currently. Luckily (and with continued research), we found that the children of the original owner were still living in our small community. The original owner's children were now in their late 80's and 90's years of age. We made a decision to call them to see if they would possess any old pictures or documentation about our house.

   The telephone call created new friends for my family. Each of the original owner's children were more than willing to help us and also extremely anxious to see what we had already completed to the home. They were very sharp and alert for their ages and very excited to see the home "where they grew up". The daughter-in-law of the original owner was the first one to visit us in the home bringing with her many pieces of information. She could still remember everything, as it was when she lived in the house. She explained to us that the first floor of the home was the only section finished during that time. The kitchen and the two bathrooms in the back of the home were added on years later. The upstairs was completely utilized as a storage area. The area of our dining room was created as a bedroom in the original home. Suddenly, she lowered her head and quietly said "Mammy died right over there, I remember it well" as she motioned toward our dining room. She explained that her mother-in-law had died of lung cancer and that they had put Mammy's bed near the windows for her.

If you recall in the previous chapter, this is the room that our entity seemed to be particularly careful of how we renovated. This is also the room we painted after a discussion about wallpapering. We later noticed that at any time we took pictures in this room there is a distinct and unexplained haze or fog in the pictures. We have yet to take a clear picture of the dining room. Yet another strange and unusual occurrence in this particular room is my wall clock. I continually reset the time on the clock, but it makes a point to stop running as if the hands of the clock were physically held to a certain time. Objects located in the room that are in the pictures that we take with a camera always seem to have a weird sense of reflection. It does not matter the time of the day that we take these pictures or if the lights are on or off. The pictures are taken with the blinds opened and closed. We just cannot produce a clear picture of this room. I begin to believe that the evidence again proved the fact that the entity was among us. The one thing that came to mind and I could not shake was that I always felt that our entity was a male.

The daughter-in-law also validated that the remainder of the house had been completed after World War II. All of the children returned from the war with families and without a place to live. Because of this, they completed the internal structure of the house and added several small living quarters. The reason behind the design was to accommodate everyone with individual privacy and to provide an opportunity for the families to get back on their feet after the war. After talking with the daughter-in-law, this gave us additional insight as to how our home might have originally looked.

She expressed that she would like to return for another visit with her husband and sister-in-law. We anxiously agreed and told her any information they may have would help with our restoration and will be greatly appreciated. We made it a point at these times to not discuss the strange occurrences that were going on in our house with her.

We started to notice quite often the aroma of the Fireplace as if it was burning logs. Many occasions we were afraid the house was on fire. We had yet to use the fireplace during this time, as we wanted to make sure the fireplace was safe enough. We finally called a professional to check the condition of the fireplace. His recommendation was not to burn wood in the fireplace due to age and the condition of the structure. He stated that the chimney of the fireplace was no longer safe. He advised us to refurbish the fireplace into gas unit, which we later did.

We explained to him about the aroma of wood smoke coming from the cavity of the fireplace. The professional made a comment that the aroma would be common in old fireplaces during a cold, damp and windy day. We explained to him that the wood smell occurs very often, even in the hot sultry days of the summer months. He smiled with a slight smirk to let us know he did not believe us, but even to this day it continues to bring into the room the smell of burning wood in other areas of the home, we experience the smell of kerosene, similar to the kerosene lamps that were once used for light and warmth. We do not own any kerosene lamps or heaters, and yet another mystery of the home that we cannot find an answer for. We have spoken with many professionals for home inspections, each time the electric, plumbing, heating, and foundation analysis checking out to be ok.

I found out the hard way not to complain too often or too loudly about working on the house. One time I recall having just about enough of the restoration projects due to stress and exhaustion. Everything seems to be going wrong and costing us much more than we had anticipated.

After complaining at the dinner table one evening, I got up from the dining room table with tears streaming down my face stacking the dirty dishes as I wept. I looked at my husband with tear-stained eyes and said, "I have had enough. I hate this house and want to sell it now!" Immediately as the words came from my lips, I turned on the garbage disposal and it literally exploded with a tremendous growl. On other occasions when we were feeling frustrated and ready to cut our losses and unload the haunted house on another unsuspecting person, we would always receive a sign from our unsuspecting guests to calm down and shut up.

Another problem we begin to notice was the door that led to the basement would never stay closed. It did not matter how many times a day we would shut the door, when we walked back into the kitchen it would be completely open. My step-dad, frustrated with the "automatic" door, installed a screen door tension spring to the door. You would think every time we opened the door it would spring back shut without any problems. It did seem to help to a point. Many times when we are in the kitchen where the door is located it will open by itself and stay half way open then very gently shut as if someone had walked up to the door.

If you are living in similar circumstances, I recommend that you consult with home maintenance professionals. You never know when the actual problem may be nothing more than a home repair. If your results are the same as ours, document them in the journal provided. Maintain receipts of the inspections, dates and times. Also document who performed the inspection. Review your records to keep yourself calm when the unexplained occurs once again.

Rick's Thoughts

When I schedule a session (reading) with someone or a group, I always recommend they bring to their session a notepad and pen. There are several reasons for this request, including and probably the main reason, is to document the messages received from their loved-ones. The funny thing about our physical and mental shell while on our earth's plan is that our capacity of past memories appears to dissolve with age. The little things that seem routine and mundane are loving memories that are clear and alert when one moves on. For example, at a scheduled session with a family the mother (who had moved on three years ago with cancer) validated the memory of a small statue in her collection. Although the son had carefully stored the collection of several hundred small statues, neither he nor his sister even thought about them. At the session, we brought out the collection as their mom relayed to me to share a certain little statue with everyone. As I held up the tiny little figure, tears rolled down the son's eyes. He later shared with me that out of the several hundred of his mother's collection; the little statue that I brought to their attention was the only one that he personally gave to her. He stated that he would have never remembered that little gift, but his mom apparently will never forget.

Researching history and experiences are keys to unlocking the mystery of your home. Start with the original homeowner, and build a reference of past families that lived in your home. If you are the home's only residents and experiencing occurrences, research the property of the home. In my career I have had situations where the home was built on property that had a unique history. For example, one of my sessions included a family that was having strange occurrences. Situations such as the covers abruptly pulled from their bed, feeling that they were being literally pushed while walking down a hall, and shadows of figures walking across a room. The family was the original owner that built the home twenty-six years ago. As I relayed messages, I felt that others that were not associated with the family were around them. We later validated that the home's property had a unique history. Research found the property several hundred years ago was occupied by an Indian settlement. I recommend starting at your local library and city records building. Become an investigator and speak with your local residents that would know about the area's history.

Research your own family tree. Sometimes our loved ones who have moved on may be trying to relay messages (as discussed in the previous chapter). Did the strange occurrences appear to start immediately from when you occupied the home? If you had occurrences happen to you before the occupation of the home that seem to parallel with those in the home, maybe a loved-one is simply trying to guide you. Again, documentation would greatly benefit future reference.

Of course, don't forget to utilize logic. Ask yourself if there is any logical explanation for the mysterious events in your home. Are the lights flickering due to an electrical problem? Are doors closing by themselves only because the frame is warped and in need of repair? Do cold spots in your home appear due to a poorly insulated window? By utilizing logic with an open mind, results can create answers.

Remember your safety and contact the expert professionals. If the lights are flickering, contact an electrician. Call a repairman to add a new doorframe. The heating and air professional could eliminate the cold air draft. But if the problems are not created by logical explanations, your open mind while learning to understand the paranormal will bring a peace of mind.

As in my co-writer's experience above, the more that you document the better your memory will assist you. Again, this is another part of the reason for creating this book especially for you. By documenting your own personal experiences, you will create a foundation for memories.

My notes as I read:

You're Not Crazy You Have A Ghost

My notes as I read:

My notes as I read:

Chapter V

Mommy, I Am Scared

The next sets of mysterious events were experiences by our children, family, friends, and even our dear family pets. I personally feel that the events that happened to the ones who were unsuspecting and innocent, now validates that what I had been visualizing and experiencing was factual and real.

My husband's youngest son was approximately three years of age during his experience with our houseguests. He is very intelligent and quite articulate for his young age. Because of a previous divorce, he visits with us every other weekend. His bedroom is uniquely decorated to accommodate his young age, complete with a small bed. Although the bedroom's decorum transmits happiness and tranquility, he refuses to sleep in the bedroom. At first my husband and I came to a conclusion that it was due To his separation from his biological mother during his infrequent visits. We also figured that at his young age of three years old, it was very traumatic for him being in an unfamiliar room every other weekend.

One weekend evening our little son fell asleep while watching a video. My husband gently picked him up and carried our sleeping angel into his bedroom and silently placed him in his bed. We stood there for a few minutes watching our darling little child sleeping peacefully, with hopes that he would sleep throughout the night. My husband and I then retired to our bedroom for the night. Suddenly around midnight I woke up to the sound of footsteps on our main stairway, which is located just outside our bedroom door. I quickly climbed out of and went to my son's bedroom to make sure that he was still in bed asleep. I was afraid that he may have climbed out of bed walking near the stairway frightened in the dark of night. I have always been fearful of this particular staircase in our home (The home has two stairways, the main stairway leads from the dining room to the upstairs foyer). When I am near the stairway, I am overcome with the feeling that someone may fall. I entered my son's room and looked toward his little bed. Sleeping safe and sound was the figure of my darling little boy. As my eyes focused more to the darkness, I noticed a strange object hovering above his bed. To my utter amazement I noticed the shape of a balloon. A couple of days before, my son had received this balloon from a friend of ours. What really startled me was the fact that the balloon was securely placed in our living room downstairs when we went to bed. For this balloon to make it into the spare bedroom upstairs it would have had to travel quite a journey. The balloon had to float through the living room area to the dining room, make a sharp right and up a winding staircase. What would make the travel even more difficult is the fact that it had to open the spare bedroom door (the last I heard balloons are not equipped with a "door open" option) make another sharp left while entering the room. The total distance for this amazing balloon would have been several hundred feet along with obstacles to overcome to reach its final destination. As my eyes stared and my mouth open in amazement, I realized the balloon was strategically hovering in the air at just the right height for my little stepson to wake up and start playing. As my stepson continued to sleep, I removed the balloon from the room. Once again while removing the balloon; I felt I was not alone in this room. I returned back to my bedroom and remained awake the rest of the night, keeping watch for anything else to happen.

Each time my young stepson stayed with us he would refuse to go into the small bedroom. One evening, after we had placed him in his bed, he woke up screaming and terrified. His screams were so piercing; my husband and I thought something terrible had happened. We quickly ran into his bedroom to find him standing in the middle of the room crying hysterically. I picked him up and hugged him while trying to calm him down enough to find out what was wrong. As he continued to sob, we checked to make sure that he was not hurt in any way. After a few minutes he begins to calm down enough to tell us "that man woke me up again."

We asked him what man he was upset about and he kept pointing to the corner of the bedroom and saying "that man." We carried him out of the bedroom and shut the door lovingly holding him as to calm him down. We tried to comfort him by telling him that he was just having a bad dream. We explained softly to him that we did not see any man in his room, and no one was walking out of his room. As that last statement was expressed to him, the doorknob to the bedroom suddenly turned and the door opened. My husband and I were both on the front lawn so fast that we didn't realize the little one was still upstairs. We ran back into the house to find him standing in the same spot with the funniest expression on his face. Needless to say we felt really bad, but he was okay. He looked up at us with his cute brown eyes and said with a laughing tone "You two are funny mommy and daddy". From then on, we knew to listen to what the children had to say about the strange home we live in.

We were starting to believe the possibility that we had more than one entity in our house. Our children kept talking about a little boy. My youngest stepson loves to play with small toy cars. Many times he would approach us to tattle on his unseen friend. He would tell us "that little boy is not sharing". During this time when he would tattle on the little boy, his brothers and sisters would not be around.

One evening my daughter and stepdaughter and I were sitting around the dining room table talking about the day's events. As we were talking, we watched in amazement a shadowy figure of a young boy skip from the kitchen through the dining room. He skipped his way to the dining room table from where we were setting and vanished. In unison, we bent down to look under the table to see if it was my youngest stepson. There was nothing under the table. We all looked at each other and confirmed what we had just seen. Then my little stepson came in from the kitchen and into the dining room. He could not have been the child we had just seen skipping into the dining room and vanishing under the table. This had all occurred in a mere few seconds, plus we would have watched him climb from under the table and into the kitchen. His little legs could not have been that quick.

Our neighbors have a little girl approximately three to four years of age. She would come over to play with my stepson. Every time she came over to play, she would ask, "Can your other little boy play too?" She would become very frustrated with us when we would ask "what other little boy?" She would answer with "your other little boy that is my size." We do not have any other small children around this age.

My son was around ten years old when we noticed that he was suddenly fascinated with the Civil War. He would constantly act out battles while playing and ask questions regarding this period of time. He started collecting things memorabilia from this era. He would look for books or anything he could find that was related to the Civil War. We also noticed included in this sudden fascination, he began to tell us that a soldier was in his bedroom (Each of our children have their own bedroom). He would wake up in the middle of the night to let us know that the soldier was in his room again. Each time we would go into the bedroom to investigate only to find an empty bedroom. I would like to comment though that each time one of my children notices someone in their room and I enter the room, I would feel tremendous pressure. My ears would pop similar to riding on an airplane. Once again, during this time I would get the feeling that I was not alone.

There are subjects my son seems to know about the Civil War that he would have otherwise not have known. He would act out battle strategies with expertise and discuss very technical things relating to the war. Finally one day I came home from work early. As I entered my home and walked up the stairs I experienced a bright ball of light (or an orb). This time I remained calm and watched it. As my eyes remained fixed to the bright object, the ball of light quit moving and began to form into a shape. As I watched with frightened curiosity, it took the shape of a young man dressed in a Civil War uniform. A grayish shadow stood in front of me, but I could clearly see the definition of his attire. He had a face that expressed sadness. I just stood there frozen in part amazement and part fright. I decided not to move (I couldn't if I had tried) and just remain calm and watch this new guest in my home. He appeared to be marching and at first did not notice me.

Suddenly his eyes looked over towards me. As he looked at me he vanished. It was obvious that this was the entity my son regularly had conversations with. My son was always concerned about him and would often place objects in his room for him. Once he put a pocket watch in his room and told us "the soldier guy lost his a long time ago." We left the pocket watch in the place where my son placed it. My son did not seem afraid of this entity. He would always respond with, "he is my friend, I want to help him."

Our dog to this day refuses to go into our basement. No matter what we do or try she refuses to enter the basement. We are not sure exactly why she is afraid (although we have ideas). Our pet dog will just slowly walk by the basement door and whimper.

My mother also has experienced something in the basement. One day she was staying with the kids at the house and decided to help me out by doing some laundry. She said while she was in the laundry room she kept hearing an unfamiliar noise. Each time she would look around her only to find herself alone in the basement. As she started up the stairs mom would hear the sound of footsteps walking behind her. Every few steps up the stairs she would turn around to see who was following her, only to find herself again alone. As she closed the basement door behind her, she decided to stay out of the basement the rest of the day. In fact, my mother decided that she would leave the laundry to me, and to this day hesitates to go downstairs.

My recommendation to you: maintain a record of things others experience in your home. It is fun to discuss these events later and it makes you feel better about sharing your experiences. If someone else is having similar experiences, then you have even more proof you are not crazy. Always listen to children they are still innocent and seem to be more perspective to these types of things.

    Today, everyone loves to come to my house in hopes something unusual will happen.

Rick's Thoughts

Probably by now you are asking yourself "Why in the world would they stay in that house? I would be moving as quickly as I moved in!" I have to admit that I truly admire my co-writer and her family for their courage and determination. Many of us would not even consider staying one night in this house. But there are two reasons why they did. The first reason is the fact that my co-writer and her husband had a dream. Their dream consisted of restoring a house together and turning it into a home. Deep inside their hearts contained a "never give up on a dream" conviction. Today, if you visit their beautiful home, you will witness the vision of success. Yes, the "house guests" are still comfortably living within, but today the dream house is replaced with a dream home. The second reason in my belief is my co-writer. My co-writer has tremendous determination when faced with a challenge, but she also is very open-minded to the paranormal. She has even experienced some personal psychic abilities. Because of her open-minded belief, I feel the occurrences within her home are understood in a clearer analysis.

This brings me to my thoughts regarding this chapter. As you were reading did you happen to notice something? If you need to do so, read the chapter once again and see if you can pick up on it.

If the audio and visual mysteries were occurring to only one person within the home, this would be considered an isolated case. Then we would focus on the person experiencing the situations. With one person we would determine many logical factors such as age, medical condition, and personality. If all logical factors were determined to be within reason, then we would concentrate on why only this particular person is solely attracted by the energies. Possible considerations may be a close association within family, personality parallels, age, and how open to paranormal possibilities is this person. Listen carefully to every detail the person relays. I would recommend documenting the details, including time, date, and place of occurrence (Another purpose of this book). With a little research, this person will help you to attain answers to the paranormal situations. Now let us review the subject of this book, my co-writer's home.

While reading this chapter, what did you notice? We have not one, but several witnessing the same events. We have an innocent three year old child, two teenage daughters with the paranormal representing the last priority on their list, a ten year old son, a three year old child not related to the family, a loving mother assisting her daughter, and the family dog. Each one unique in personality and interest, but each experiencing the same unexplained energies within the home. So what do each individual have in common other than the shared experiences?

Each individual possess an open-minded thought and innocence. Very young children are in my belief the clearest of mind to the ones who have moved on. As a child, their young minds are still open to accept what they "see and hear". As the child continues to age, they are trained to consider it as "coincidence, creativity, and imagination", thus learning to close their mind to unexplained occurrences. Although the teenage daughters normally would brush off an unexplained event as being "freakish and weird but not real", these two were still open- minded enough to consider the possibility of energy. Mothers are unique as their minds are wrapped in the care of family. Along with the love and affection of a mother, she is still blessed with a unique ability (or intuition) and a sense of an open mind. Even an animal is very open- minded along with acute senses. Watch the mannerisms of an animal right before a storm, an impending danger, or when someone is approaching the front door.

    A key to finding answers of unexplained occurrences is simply to maintain an open mind. Accept what you see, hear, smell, and feel. Document in detail each event and review and research the documentation together. Set up a plan to share with one another any experiences, while expressing to each member of the home to feel comfortable about sharing their experience. Recall each detail of the experience, what was seen and heard. Eventually, you will find a feeling of comfort and acceptance in the home. Quite possibly, you may be the one to assist your own "house guests" with their messages. Keep an open mind...and you will understand more.

My notes as I read:

My notes as I read:

My notes as I read:

My notes as I read:

Chapter VI

The Face In the Steam and Other Physical Experiences

Although my family and friends experienced strange things in my home, I still had that annoying thought in my head "Am I Going Crazy" each time something new and strange occurred. By accident I received my first physical evidence. My teenage daughter (who by the way does not place Science as her favorite subject in school) as a school project had a Science experiment for the school's Science Fair. She had not attributed much effort into the project, and at the last minute decided to find the simplest experiment she could find. To this day I still do not know what she was trying to achieve with this particular experiment. I do know that she was supposed to boil water and add salt etc. She was instructed to take pictures of each step and put them on a poster board. When I got the pictures developed we got a real surprise. Our ghost showed up in them. The entity was the original owner and builder of our home. There was no mistake about it. He showed up as plain as he could in the steam. Also two other faces showed up in the steam as well. We still have not been able to identify these two. We were excited and freaked out at the same time. We could not see anything unusual at the time the pictures were taken. I went back to the library and checked out the book I had before with the picture of our homes first owner so I could compare the pictures.

He was a perfect match. We decided finally share some of the odd things that went on in our home with our co-workers and showed our neighbors the photos. We wanted to see if they could see what was showing up in these pictures. Everyone immediately could see the faces and were stunned. After very much prompting from all our neighbors we decided to contact the ghost's daughter-in-law to show her the photo. She agreed to come over and wanted to bring her husband and sister-in-law this time. They wanted to see their childhood home again. They all came over and we gave them the tour of what we had done to their home. They were all very pleased that we seemed to love and cherish this house as much as their family did many years ago. After the tour we were very apprehensive about bringing up the picture and I think my husband and I had decided not to say anything. Finally the daughter in law said I want to see these pictures. We brought them out and she immediately said that is him. She showed it to her sister-in-law and with tears in her eyes she said "that is my dad." She also told us not to be afraid he was a gentle sort of man and loved children. We now not only had physical evidence but we also had confirmation from his family. We started looking a lot closer at other photos we had and started noticing faces in them too. There were also fogs streaks of light and sometimes orbs in many of the pictures we had.

My friends who now were all intrigued by the things going on in my house kept daring me to put a tape recorder somewhere and see if any voices showed up (they had seen this done on a TV show). I was very reluctant to try this. I don't know why but I just didn't think I was brave enough for this. Finally after much prompting I tried it. On the night I decided to do this we did not have any of the kids in the house. I put the tape recorder in my stepson's room at the top of the stairs. We did not hear anything unusual that night. The next morning we played the tape back and we got a voice. The voice sounded like that of an elderly man. What he said was "you need to go to Elmer's." We had many of our friends listen to this and everyone couldn't believe it. We decided to have it analyzed by a computer expert. He did many experiments on the tape and came to the conclusion that this did not match anyone in my family's voice. We told him it was just my husband and I home at the time this was taped. He came to the conclusion that this was a third voice. He also explained that the computer picked up something else. Someone had walked on the staircase at one point on the tape but it could not have finished all the way up or down. It just took a few steps on the stairs and then the sound vanished. He was amazed too. We decided to have the ghost's daughter-in-law listen to what we had. By this time she wanted to find out the reason her father-in-law was still in the house. She listened to the tape and did not know who "Elmer" was at the time. About a week later she was knocking on my door with a big smile. She said I know who "Elmer" is. She explained that Elmer's Grocery Store used to adjoin our property and she thought he was referring to the Grocery Store. We were greatly surprised to have the mystery solved. Now many of our ghost's ancestors just stop by the house to visit. We feel are all welcome and have a kind of bond with them.

My mother was staying with my children on another occasion when she had an eerie experience with a balloon. We think our little boy ghost loves balloons. Sometime we just buy them now for him and put them around the house. Whenever there is a balloon in the house we can usually track our smallest ghost. On this occasion my mother and daughter were watching TV in the family room when they noticed the helium balloon my son had received come up the backstairs. My son had left this in the kitchen. At first they didn't think too much about it. Then the balloon came down from the ceiling to the height of a small child. The balloon did not move up and down or even side to side. They described what they witnessed to be like a child running around the house in circles with a balloon. It looked like he was not only running but also skipping and playing with this balloon all over the house. The balloon would hold still for a while then go down the stairs then backs up. It would do circles then stop.

To make it more ominous they said the string attached to the balloon looked like it was being held and pulled by the middle of the string. My mother who at the time didn't like these experiences too well was scared to death. She sat on our couch and put my kids on there with her and made them stay there. They were not to leave the room. As soon as I got home they all started yelling for me to come upstairs. The balloon was still doing its tricks. We decided to run the tape recorder to see if we could pick anything up. We noticed that when the balloon came close to us the temperature in that spot dropped considerable. Anyways we turned on the tape for a while to see what we might get. At one point the balloon seemed to have been released. When we played back the tape we got a small voice saying, "Get my balloon." Sometimes we just take pictures in different places in the house to see what will show up. We get a lot of things we are not sure what they are. They just show up in the photos. I have never been able to get anything on a tape but the two incidences I have just described. I have not tried to hard either. Out of all the evidence I have these two bother me the most.

The voices sound hollow. It was a great experience to capture this, but it also seemed rather sad to me. I know the little boy had no idea he is a ghost.

Do not be afraid to try to get physical evidence. It not only will help identify who is in our house but also may calm your nerves. If you are like we were your imagination can run away with you. We were very glad to find out our entity just loved his home. We did not have to worry about this entity anymore. In the beginning I thought maybe a serial killer or someone had killed a whole family in my house. Our entity is just there partly I feel because he not only loved the home he built but his memories are there. He seems very content to be in our home with my family there.

Keep copies of any pictures you have. Fill out the journal with anything that you may have noticed when the photos or evidence was acquired. Also make copies of any tapes or videos with anything you might capture. I just now realize how lucky I am for having these experiences. You will probably come to the same conclusion.

Photos courtesy of the author

Rick's Thoughts

If you are reading this book based on the fact that you are living in a home with "house guests", then hopefully by now you realize several similarities to your own situation. Although it may seem that you are living in a home that may be defined as "one of a kind", you will find that the paranormal activities are very similar to those who reside in a paranormal home. Shadows appearing from the hallway, mists or fog like entities gliding down the stairway, strange sounds from another room, physical objects displaced by an unseen force, and concrete responses from an invisible energy are all common messages from loved-ones who have moved on. If you recall in a previous chapter, we examined the reasons for energies to communicate by way of a physical attraction. They are simply expressing a need to relay a message. Again I do not believe the energy's plan is to bring any harm to those residing in the home. They want to acknowledge their existence to you. If you attend a function as the guest of honor and enter the room, do you quickly run and hide under a coffee table or in a corner as to not be seen? The answer is no of course; instead you would enter through the front door with a smile and a handshake. The same are with energies that have moved -on. Now let us change that scenario to a different concept. If you attend a function, but want to remain inconspicuous as to avoid the limelight, what would you do? My answer to this question is most likely you would sneak in the back door, silently sneak over to a corner of the room the farthest away from the guest of honor, and graciously acknowledge your presence if absolutely necessary.

    The same are with energies who have moved-on. Their purpose on earth is to simply guide us in our earth's plan. They do not want to be the "guest of honor" and search for the limelight. At the same time, they understand that when necessary, the tools of physical evidence are to be utilized to So if they are simply trying to relay messages and not trying to scare the heck out of you, what steps should you take to best understand the messages? My fellow co-writer and I have pointed out several steps to take in previous chapters that I believe you will find are tremendous tools. This chapter shares with you an additional tool that will greatly benefit your understanding of your mysterious situation. If you have a camera, place it in area of the home that can be easily attained when needed. Again remember that the energies decide when physical evidence is necessary, but like they say a picture is worth a thousand words. As in the chapter you have just read, the photographs not only achieved physical evidence to the homeowner, but also brought comfort and faith to the original owner's family. Reflect on the message. Do you not think that the original owner appeared in the picture of the science project because he "oops, I got caught"? I do not believe so. If you recall, part of the science project included photographs of a pot of steam. This was the perfect time for the energy of the original owner to appear in physical

evidence to acknowledge whom he was, why he was in the home, and validation for his family.
He was simply "standing in the corner away from the guest of honor, but acknowledged his presence when necessary".

A tape recorder device is another tool that may come in handy, although evidence obtained by audio is at times very rare. Communication by those who have moved-on are different then while on our earth's plan. On earth when we communicate when your mouth opens and your lips move. A sound resonates in the form of speech, and dialects are understood based on the demographic region. When I relay messages from the energies who have moved-on, I have noticed a different type of communication. During sessions the energy of loved-ones communicate to me in different forms that is necessary for that particular session. They may communicate by simply relay messages by thought or what I call "visual messages to the mind". Another way of communication is by energy of bright light that appears. Yet another way is by actually relaying to me a visual of the energy as they appeared during their earth's plan. The last example seems to be utilized as to validate to their loved-ones their actual presence.

Based on my experience, the communication from a spiritual energy is unique in that the "sound" is more of a "spiritual thought". Physical sound becomes unnecessary as communication is acquired by a feeling and a thought. For example, as you are reading the words of this book you can "feel" the emotion and imagine my co-writer speaking to you the words she has written. Physically, she and I are not setting in the room with you at this moment sharing our experiences. Yet, your thoughts and emotions while reading the book create an atmosphere as if we were actually there in your home. The same is true for communication with energies. You can communicate by feelings and an open mind (review the previous chapter if you prefer). But again the energies from those who have moved on are very acute to how and what is the best way to communicate messages to us. At times, audio sound may be the preferred option. So, if sounds are being experienced, record them.

A balloon moving across the room by an invisible force is another example of validations for a message translation. Objects moved from one end of a cabinet to another end, a picture of a loved one slightly turned around, missing objects suddenly appearing in another area of a home are some of the many examples I have heard that occur. Once again, it is merely a communication process. The loved one's objective is not to harm or to frighten, but rather to communicate. They have your attention, now listen for the message.

My notes as I read:

My notes as I read:

My notes as I read:

My notes as I read:

Chapter VII

Family Togetherness Creates Family Solutions

After all that we had been through with our unique house, the decision of learning to live and adjust was a major concern. Our experiences in our home went totally against the ways that our own parents had raised us to believe. The occurrences of our home continued to also go against the beliefs of my husband and I as well, but we had mentally and physically experienced the home's visitors. As many reasons why we tried to tell ourselves that this cannot be, we knew that we had to come to terms with our reality. The experiences of our home were real, and it was not imagination by one person. This was very difficult for me because of the strong beliefs shared with me by my dear grandmother's strong Christian beliefs. I can still to this day hear her stern but gentle voice referencing the paranormal as "works of the devil".

Personally, I have never felt all of the things that occur in my home can be defined as of the devil". The experiences that I have become a part of have created quite an opposite decision. Today, when the opportunity within my home allows me to see a spirit or ghost, I am reminded of the promise of life-after- death. I feel my family actually bonds on some unique type of level with our home's entities. At one point, after reviewing all documentation, we sat down as a family and came to the conclusion that we did not want to move from our home. We love our home, including all the out –of-the-ordinary experiences. I think because my husband and I were equally open to the strange happenings, this actually helped our children. I have no doubt if we had expressed an emotion of hopeless terror in front of our children, we would have expressed to our children that we did not have faith within. In our case our entities seemed friendly but lost or in need of direction. Our family made a decision, to make our home a home and to assist these entities in the way that they wanted us to. We expressed to the children we were living in a special type of situation and most people would not believe them. A positive note is that our children never have the chance to say "I'm Bored". If they do, we place a flashlight in their hand and suggest they go on a ghost hunt. We have found that by keeping our responses light and sometimes humorous, our children accept their unique domain in a comfortable setting.

Utilize this journal to write down your family's individual pros and cons for staying in your house. If you decide moving from the home is the best solution for your family, then by all means do so.
Remember, a haunted house is not for everyone, but the love of a bonded family is for everyone.

Rick's Thoughts

A family is to work together, share together, worship together, and be together as one. We have all been in our own unique circumstances within our family. It may or may not be as unique as my co-writers experience, but we have all at one time or another had our experiences. The key to this whole chapter is family unity. You alone cannot travel life's curves and cliffs. You alone cannot find a total solution to life's trials and tribulations. You alone cannot determine which key will fit the right door. You are not alone as a part of a family, and one person should not determine family decisions.

I have worked with several families like my co-writers that are "searching for answers". On the average, one family member will contact me for assistance or solutions. Although one family member will make the initial contact, the other family members will acknowledge the occurrences but will nominate the one family member to find the answers. I have heard many reasons why only the one family member will contact me. These reasons include:

- I see and hear the occurrences, but do not believe they are of the paranormal
- I do not want to be involved
- I was raised to believe that this is "of the devil" and should not be acknowledged

- I do not want our friends and neighbors to think we are crazy
- Maybe it will just go away

Finally, after a continuation of the strange and unnatural occurrences, a family member will contact me to "just see if I feel anything". This was also the case of my co-writer. Although her family knew that their home was anything but normal, she was the only one initially to contact me. I can recall the first session at her home. Her children were not present per my request. I wanted to make sure that I did not "lead" feedback from their experiences at this time. I can still remember her husband's expression on his face when I entered their home. A very outgoing and charismatic person, he seems to send me an "I know things are going on, but I am not sure about this stuff" look. He casually walked along with me, but did not express a believable persona. As we continued through the session, I begin to notice his casual attitude became more and more involved. I do know one thing about him; he was genuinely concerned about his family's well-being. By the end of the evening, he became a valuable assistant for me, and continues to be to this day.

Children are a very valuable part of family. Children are true blessings of a family given to us by our creator. Children's input to a family should not be ignored. As parents, we should learn to really listen to our children in every situation. In regards to paranormal situations within the home, I recommend that you listen even more.

Based on my experience, I feel that children are more perceptive to the paranormal. When we are created into our earthly shell, our mind and soul is pure of thought and perception. As we grow older, society raises us to consider things as "coincidence, imagination, and even ignorance". Some of our (I surmised that I am one), abilities continue to remain and overcome the objections. I have been defined as stubborn, but I define myself as "listening to my inner creation". Children have the unique ability to "listen without prejudice". As a family, their abilities are valuable in unique situations regarding the paranormal. In a paranormal situation, I feel that you should allow your children to be open with their thoughts and feelings. For example if they state that they "saw a shadow walking across the hallway", allow them to tell you what they saw exactly, how they felt when they saw the apparition, and any sounds they may have heard. Do not force them to respond, but at the same time let he or she knows that it is ok to share with you. At the same time, I feel that you should not force your thoughts and beliefs onto them either, especially very young children.

When first experiencing a paranormal experience within the home, I would recommend that initially the adults within the family review the possible solutions without interaction from the younger siblings.

Possible solutions were pointed out within this book, such as moving from the residence, contacting professional advice, etc. After consideration of the best solution for the family, allow the younger siblings to be a part of the decision. For example, if the solution will be to move from the residence, sit down together as a family and share the reasons why. Again this should be from all adults (father/mother etc.) and not by just one. They should understand that the decision is a "shared" decision. If the solution is to contact a professional (such as a psychic medium, etc.), share with the children what will be the next step. Again on the first initial visit of the professional, I would not allow the younger ones to be present. This will allow you to determine if the professional is a confident solution, if the professional is viable, and if the professional will be able to bring comfort into the home. Once these have been determined, I would share with the younger ones in a positive manner the steps toward bringing comfort and acceptance into the home. Be sure and document what your children are relaying to you as you continue to reach the comfort of your home. This will be a valuable documentation for future reference.

Maintaining family unity in any situation is a bond so strong that any and all can be accomplished. Utilize this bond if you are experiencing a unique situation.

Love within the family will be your biggest asset.

My notes as I read:

You're Not Crazy You Have A Ghost

My notes as I read:

You're Not Crazy You Have A Ghost

My notes as I read:

My notes as I read:

Chapter VIII

A Call To the PI (Paranormal Investigator)

Now that I was sure my house was haunted and we were just crazy enough to stay living in it, I wanted to know why my home was haunted. A few days after my family decided to stay in the home, I was listening to local radio station advertising an up-coming "Physic Fair" in a town near ours. My mother and I decided we would attend the fair to "check it out". Either one of us had any past experience with a psychic or someone specializing in the paranormal.

Before the experiences in our home, mother and I did not fully believe in the psychic ability. I gathered up some of the pictures I had that captured paranormal spirit activity (at least this was the only answer we had at the time) that were captured in my home and took them with us to the fair. When we arrived at the Physic Fair it was absolutely over- whelming. There were a variety of books relating to the paranormal, crystals, and different herbs and potions. We thought it was all kind of weird. Among the books, crystals, and herbs, were several tables set up for those claiming to have a psychic gift. Several of the apparent psychics indicated they had very special gift for being able to know certain things.

We had no idea how to choose the physic to consult, or if we even wanted to bother. After walking down a few more isles of tables, we came upon an information desk. My mother and I proceeded to ask which person would be best to ask questions about hauntings. They directed us to a specific booth of a physic. We walked over to the location of the booth and waited for our turn to meet with the person setting behind the table. As we approached the physic, she asked us to write what we wanted to know about on a small piece of paper. I wrote on the paper "Is my house haunted?" As she read the question on the paper, she proceeded with a very typical answer "Your home is haunted by a previous owner etc." It was a very generic and disappointed reading. How many homes in America are stated as haunted by previous owners? Would your answer be most of them? At the end of our uneventful reading, I shared with the physic the pictures we had taken of our ghostly visitor. As her eyes looked down that the photos in her hand, she became suddenly very excited. The psychic instructed us to remain right where we were standing as she was going to show them to her supervisor. I did not know that psychics had supervisors. Ok, back to the experience, the psychic shared the photos with another lady who examined the pictures with the same response. In a matter of minutes, a crowd gathered of every physic in the building examining my pictures.

The pictures had grabbed the attention of everyone at the fair, and the next thing I knew everyone in the place was examining the pictures with a thought or an idea.

They asked if I would consider scheduling a psychic group to visit my home in order to perform a study. I agreed with a slight hesitation, believing the whole time that the study of my home would never surface.

Approximately two weeks from when we attended the fair, I received a call from the original psychic I had met with during my visit. She proceeded with excitement to request an invitation for a party of ten to twelve physics to come over to my house for a study. I agreed with some hesitation, as I was still a little bit skeptical of this whole situation. After pausing a few moments to decide if I actually wanted this strange group in my home, I decided that it might actually be a little bit fun. The one thing I did know at this point was that I did not totally believe in all of this paranormal mumbo-jumbo. I proceeded to devise a plan to have some of my family during their visit for ease of mind and security. My plan was to have a family member escort a few members of the psychic group while they toured my home. I did not want them wondering around the house with one of us looking at picture or objects in my home and coming up with stories. As the psychic party arrived, I was introduced to each one. The party included psychics from four different Midwestern states.

Included in the group were physics that specialized in assisting with law enforcement and detectives researching cases of missing children. Other physics in the group specialized in specific fields, such as physic photography. As the group shared their thoughts with me, I quickly surmised that some were definitely more genuine than others. Almost immediately upon entering my home the psychics sensed paranormal activity. Two lady psychics in particular especially impressed me. They were describing ghostly activities and situations that I had experienced. The ghosts they described were what my family had actually witnessed themselves. Other psychics in the group were not as convincing, in fact you might describe them as just plain weird. I was also quite amused that it seems to be a competition of sorts, as one psychic would try and portray to be better in the field than the other. One psychic in particular scared me so much that after the group left I begin sleeping with the lights on. A few days after the group of physics had left I began to calm down from the experience and realized that some of the things described to me were just from a very over active imagination. I decided to only believe in what I had experienced in my home.

   A few weeks later I received in the mail a photo album with pictures they had took. Many of them had apparitions in them or unexplained fogs. I now had additional photos to add to my home visitors collection.

   I was fortunate that I found out Rick possessed the unique ability to communicate with spirits. Several years ago, Rick and I had worked together for a company and when I brought pictures of our "visitors" to the office, he seemed to be very interested in them. After I had told everyone about my adventure with the physics, Rick asked if he could come over and see my house. At the time I was not aware of Rick's physic ability, but agreed to let him have a tour. I assumed he was curious about the house being haunted like so many others. I figured that he must have been yet another visitor wanting to see if my family was crazy. Needless to say, I was very pleasantly surprised when Rick explained the reason he requested a tour. He told me he had always had the ability to communicate with spirits. At this time, he was not very open about his ability, and actually didn't want any of our other co- workers to know. He came over and described things perfectly as they had happened. He immediately made contact with our Civil War soldier.

Later, Rick asked my son questions that were being relayed to him by my unseen spirit. My son seemed to know everything he was talking about. I felt so relieved after Rick's visit, especially when he explained we had several entities within the home and that he did not feel any harm from them. I had suspected this and was very grateful for the validation. It was also good to have someone I knew and trusted to be helping me with my unusual home.

Rick continues to this day to follow up with my home's entities. We have even been able to form a unique type of friendship and comfort with the energies in my home with Rick's assistance.

If you do not know a physic, just ask others. You never know who may have abilities or might know someone who is a psychic medium. For me it was a wonderful experience to find a friend who could help. The journal at the end of this book is provided for you to document notes of experiences or messages that a physic or paranormal professional might share with you during a visit. Remember not all psychics are genuine. Write down your notes and utilize your common sense on what they tell you. If they are telling you stories you have never experienced, chances are they are not the real things. If the psychics share knowledge that appears to match your experiences listen very carefully, document, and review your notes. By documenting in a journal, the questions that your family experiences in your home will dissipate and replace with comfort and acceptance.

Rick's Thoughts

"What is a true physic?" I have heard this question many times. As is in any industry, you have your "good" with the 'bad". In the medical profession, a doctor or nurse's expertise is based on years of practice and education. In the business segment, a person's expertise is based on his company's financial success and how high he or she "climbed the ladder". In any industry, certain criteria will determine the 'expertise' within that field. But also within any industry, a few will often taint this field of expertise. For example, in the medical profession a nurse or doctor who states, "expert advice" only to later announce that their background is not as viable as stated, creates distrust within the profession. In the business segment, ones who sit at the top of the ladder and creates a portfolio of "amazing success" only to find the "books were shuffled to hide the corruption", creates distrust for business. The paranormal industry is not exempt from the "good" with the "bad". I will be the first to admit to this day I at times wish to remain anonymous about my abilities, due to the negative media. Many of so-called psychics have been caught and found that greed was in fact their established motive. Let's face it; the paranormal is a very unique product with a limited number of those who believe in life everlasting. But there are also those who are truly genuine, and is dedicated to "helping those here and there".

My recommendation? Very simple really. As my co-writer stated, document the messages that the physic relays to you. Are they generic messages? Are they messages to scare you into more appointments with him or her, or are they expressing a comfort? Most importantly, are they requesting a monetary amount that does not actually bring to you any return of value. Do they request additional monies after the appointment? Basically, our creator gave us the gift of choice and common sense; utilize these gifts for what is best for you.

You're Not Crazy You Have A Ghost

My notes as I read:

My notes as I read:

My notes as I read:

My notes as I read:

Chapter IX

Lessons Of Understanding

With the help of Rick, my family has not only accepted that our house is haunted but we have learned how to co-habitat with our entities. Rick visits my home frequently to communicate with our ghosts. I contact him especially when the strange things seem to be occurring most often. Usually when we notice occurrences taking place, this is our cue that they want to communicate with us.

Some of the ghosts we have in our home (such as the Civil War soldier or the original owner) made their personalities known to us by their actions. Others in my home are not as easy to detect why they are there. Each time Rick arrives to communicate with our entities, more of the reasons why they are there, what they would like to express and even who they are become validated.

I am the type of person who has to know everything I can about each entity so that I can be comfortable with the situation. I do not think I will ever know why we have so many entities in our house.

All of the psychics that have inspected my house describe a type of port hole in one of our four bedrooms. Each psychic expert has explained that by our acceptance of the ghosts, we have opened up a place in our home for them to come for help. My first thought was not to believe this theory. But with each day's new experiences, I have become more convinced this may be true. None of our entities (other than the original owner) have any ties to our house or property that we have found. With Rick's help I have made the decision to not be frightened but rather help each one of them the best of my own abilities. I always believe if this was one of my deceased relatives, I would want someone to do the same for them. In every case that we have been able to communicate, our entities have all relayed to us that they did not move on because they felt they did not deserve to go into the light. I am happy to say that I believe we have assisted two entities into the light.

   Our Civil War ghost was the first that we assisted. He was very sad as I had described in an earlier chapter. He relayed to us (through Rick's abilities) that he had killed a couple of men during the war, and felt that he was not worthy to move forward due to these acts. This is the entity that my son liked so well. He had made a real connection with our Civil War ghost. On one of Rick's visits with this entity he asked my son to describe what this ghost looked like.

   My son described what I had seen perfectly. Rick asked him to later draw a picture of this ghost. The next day my son drew a beautiful picture of his Civil War friend. He then took a yellow marker and colored the picture yellow all around the ghost's portrait and wrote the words "Bye" in the corner. I asked why he did this, in which my son replied "He might go into the light soon and I will miss him." I was so impressed by my son and how calm he appeared to be with this whole situation. I went out and bought a frame for his artwork. We hung the picture on the wall in his room. I bought an inexpensive frame, and for some reason the picture fell from the wall and broke. I planned to purchase another frame and hang it back up but didn't get to it right away. I had put the picture in a dresser drawer in my son's room for safe keeping. One day when we came home from shopping my son went into his room and came out yelling at me to see what our Civil War ghost "Garrison" had done. I quickly rushed up to his room and there lying in the middle of his floor was the portrait he drew. It was covered up with some toys that were in his room. Everything was piled up neatly in the middle of the floor, with the artistic picture lying face-up underneath the organized pile. We pulled the picture out from under the toys and found a frame to display Garrison's portrait once again in his room. To this day the picture remains displayed on the wall in my son's room.

I contacted Rick about this occurrence and we scheduled a time for him to visit my home. Before Rick's arrival, my son started asking a lot of questions again about the Civil War era. He had a book that he was looking at and wanted to know why in one particular picture a soldier was getting ready to shoot another soldier that was lying down on the ground. I did not know how to answer the question except to tell him this was war and things like this happen. He replied that this was how Garrison was shot. I asked my son how he would know this in which he replied that he did not exactly know the answer to the question.

When Rick arrived for his visit, we did not inform him of my son's discussion about the picture in the book. The first thing Rick relayed to us when he started to communicate with this entity was that he had been killed jut like my son and I had discussed. Rick asked if we had been looking at a book. We acknowledged that we had and showed him what we had talked about. He explained that "Garrison" had been able to put his actual death out of his thoughts until that moment.

Once we started discussing it he remembered it all. He also recalled the pain he felt and that his feet were wet. He also relayed how bad he missed his wife. He also realized how much my son really cared about him. He told us he was ready to move on soon.

One night my son said Garrison tapped him on his shoulder and that he knew he was going to move on. After that night we have never seen our Civil War soldier again. My son still remembers him fondly and brings him up often. He always says I hope Garrison is happy now. My son, Rick and I felt like we had helped someone who had needed it for over 100 years. We do not think of these spirits as ghosts anymore but more as family. This was worth all the sleepless nights and being scared. It reaffirmed that what we had decided to do was the right decision.

    Almost immediately after "Garrison" moved on we begin smelling cigarette smoke. We could not figure out where this was coming from. This went on for several weeks and I decided to call Rick. This time Rick came with a mutual friend of ours who was curious. She was dating a State Police Detective and he also wanted to come over. Rick made contact with our smoker right away. He explained this entity had died of lung cancer a few years earlier. He also relayed that he came from a small town in Arkansas. He was able to get his name along with the name of the small town. He told us that this entity felt bad because his death was very long and painful for his family. He now felt like if he would have quit smoking he could have spared them so much pain. The entity relayed that his daughter was getting married soon and he wanted her to know that he knew and would be with her. Our Police Detective took down all the information and stated that he would check it out. He was able to find the small town in Arkansas and even a family by the name we had been given. Rick wrote to the family anonymously to relay the loved one's message. About a week later we never smelled the smoke or felt the presence of this ghost again. Never forget the experiences and I recommend again that you document every detail. My personal feelings are that these experiences that I have shared with you in this chapter were very spiritual to me. Embrace the feeling of accomplishment when you have been able to help someone, even if you can't see them. Carry the feeling of wanting to be of help not only the dead, but the living. If we did this every day we would all feel a sense of life fulfilled.

Rick's Thoughts

The heavens and the earth are a creation given to us as a gift. The gift was for our unique energy to live upon forever, as stated in the book of Genesis (King James Version). So the question remains, when we move on do we go to a "heaven" or do we end? Throughout the history of man, this question has been a subject of debate based on belief. Continually controversial, but never without the ingredient of intrigue. I feel that when one moves on, he is again given the "choice". The choice to remain on the creation called earth to guide and protect those that they love, and to "move forward" at a time chosen. Some may define moving forward as "going toward the light" or "entering the light", with each and all having the same meaning. I feel that when one feels that his choice is to "move forward"; one again has the gift of "choice". As in the case of the energy described in this chapter, He felt that although his loved ones had "moved forward", his need to remain on the earth was his decision. I feel that when we move on, we are loved so by our creator that our energy is given the opportunity to continue our life's path in a way we feel is most needed. A gift of choice.

As in the case of my friend and co-author's experiences, I feel that we can encounter those that are not connected to us, but will communicate to us in order to reach those who are in earth's plan. The "smoker" is such an example. Although he was not connected to the home owner in any way, he understood the opportunity to "reach his loved ones". By validating his presence with a physical validation (smell of smoke), he was able to connect with the home owner. Of course, if the home owner had been ignoring the occurrences within the home, his opportunity would have been mute. Fortunately, the home owner has learned to "Listen", and therefore made a connection. We then were able to acknowledge and validate his message, and reach those that he loved so.

I personally do not completely understand the presence of what some would define as portals. My personal believe is that there is not a "portal" or "door" that those who have moved on, but rather an "opportunity" to come through and share messages for a reason. I have worked with many who have entities within their home that is not directly connected to the home's current owner. But with the ability to "Listen", I found the loved ones are connected in some way. They may be connected to the home, the property, or simply the ability of the ones within the home. To those who have moved on, I feel that their portal is simply a memory placed on earth during their life's path. A portal is an opportunity to connect to those who will "Listen".

So what should you do if the unknown is being experienced within your home? My recommendation is to utilize the tools that we have shared with you in previous chapters of this book. Document and record every detail, including how you feel during the experience.

Acknowledge the presence, and contact one who has the ability to relay messages. Ask for guidance and comfort. Most importantly understand that it is of no harm, but rather an opportunity for you to share messages.

My notes as I read:

You're Not Crazy You Have A Ghost

My notes as I read:

My notes as I read:

You're Not Crazy You Have A Ghost

My notes as I read:

My notes as I read:

Chapter X

Now Let Us Review

Below are highlights and a brief review of each chapter. Utilize these next few pages as a "quick reference" during your own experiences.

- What you are experiencing in your home is unique, but not rare.
- To accept will bring comfort.
- Your experiences are simply energies (spirits) that are now in life-everlasting. While on earth's plan they were just like you.
- A home is created with loving memories that remain within the energies.
- You have nothing to fear but fear itself, and to understand will eliminate the fear
- You have the ability of perception. Work with it, and the understanding along with the communication will become much easier.
- "Physical Messages" do not portray harm.
- "Physical Messages" are simply a way for the energies to get your attention in order to relay a message.
- Do not allow yourself to over-imagine, but rather be open- minded with logic.

- When you expect a presence, ask yourself what do you feel, and why do you feel this way.
- When a "physical message" occurs, ask yourself if there is any possible logical reason.
- When all logic is acknowledged and can be nothing other than a paranormal, ask yourself "what is the message?"
- Do not ignore the "physical messages".
- The more you accept and acknowledge the presence, the less the "physical messages" will occur.
- Once again, utilize logic for each occurrence.
- Check the home for any logical reasons such as electrical, plumbing, or insulation problems.
- Contact a professional (such as an electrician, plumber, etc.) to assist in establishing any logical solutions.
- Keep in mind that the energies really do not want to be the "guest of honor".
- They intentions are not to disrupt your earthly life, but merely to assist with guidance.
- Physical messages are not to scare you, but rather to get your attention in order to guide.
- Document, Document, Document!

- Document the date, time, occurrence, names of witnesses, and thoughts during the occurrence.
- Photograph and or sound record the occurrence.
- Research past history of the home, the land, and even the history of the area itself.
- Research the family history of the previous owners – build a reference library.
- Research your own family history.
- You're a family, work together, share together, worship together, and just be together.
- Do not try to handle the situation alone.
- At the same time, establish a "team leader" in the family to establish and to organize.
- By all means include the children and assist them to understand.
- Allow them to be open with their individual thoughts.
- Spend time to review your documentation as a family.
- As you review, express acceptance and comfort.
- Initially, the adults should review the experience to consider all options. Once options are reviewed, accept the children

into the discussion (if they have experienced themselves).
- Ask the question, "is this occurring to one member of the family or many in the family?"
- If the occurrence is related to one person, determine the logical factors such as age, medical condition, and personality.
- If all the above are within reason, determine why energies are communicating with that one person only.
- Document his/her details.
- Listen to your children, as they are the most perceptive.
- Don't forget your pets.
- Your pet's senses are far more sensitive than a human being.
- If the option of scheduling a psychic medium is discussed, research the background of the medium.
- Review third party opinions regarding the medium.
- If the medium is a "payment medium" review the overall value.
- When a psychic medium is scheduled, recommend that your children not be present.
- Open your mind.

- Acknowledge what you see, hear, smell, and feel.
- Listen
- Keep the faith

My notes as I read:

You're Not Crazy You Have A Ghost

My notes as I read:

My notes as I read:

My notes as I read:

My notes as I read:

Chapter XI

A Final Word

Although this may be the final chapter in this book/journal, it is just the beginning of many memorable experiences for you. If you read this book due to your own personal paranormal situations within your home, my co-writer and I hope that we have been able to assist you in some way to reach your comfort goals and acceptance. Continue to learn toward understanding your experiences and challenges. Maintain your faith and ask for guidance. Research the experience together as a family, and strengthen the bond. Continue to document your experiences within this book or in a journal. Review and read the book as many times as need be.

You may have read this book simply out of sheer curiosity, or may have an interest in the paranormal. The value in knowledge is to maintain an open mind to that which is unknown. All great philosophers, inventors, and leaders have achieved goals beyond imagination just by thinking the impossible with an open mind. Today we take for granted the many material inventions and words of profound wisdom that has changed our lives, all from the thoughts of an open mind. We hope that after you have read this book, you too will open your mind to the many messages that are around us.

In summary, my co-writer and I want to thank you for the opportunity to share the experiences and the faith of life everlasting. Life is full of wonders, trials, memories, adjustments, and surprises. This book is just an example. The experience began as a trial of sanity, belief, and surprises. Later, it became a series of wonders, adjustments, and understanding. The final result was that of comfort, faith, and guidance. As you continue through your path in life, never take for granted what may be an amazing wonder in life everlasting.
Keep the faith.

You're Not Crazy You Have A Ghost

My notes after I read:

My notes after I read:

My notes after I read:

My notes after I read:

Bonus Chapter I

The Nursery For Our New Arrival

After living in our home for a few years, we were excited to announce that I was pregnant with my third child. The pregnancy unfortunately was a very difficult one. My doctor advised me to be placed on bed rest for at least six months of my pregnancy period. Being medically advised and placed on bedrest can be difficult for anyone, but living in a haunted house is an added weird experience. I was put on medication to keep me from going into premature labor. The medicine made me feel restless and I was awake a lot more than I could sleep. I would be home alone during the day, or at least I thought I was. I would hear all sorts of sounds and didn't know where they were coming from. This went on at all times during the day and night. For whatever reason I would often fall asleep around 10 am and sleep for only intervals of a few hours.

One day I woke up extremely cold. It was so frigid that I could actually to see my breath. I arose out of bed and ventured over to the thermostat to check to see if there may be a problem with the home's furnace. I slowly walked to the other rooms on the second floor to find each were toasty warm. For some strange reason, the only cold spot appeared to be my bedroom. The windows and doors of the house were never opened during this time. The cold air in my bedroom lasted for a short time, and just as quickly as it had dropped in temperature, it returned to the warmth of the other rooms. I will say that I never felt like I was ever alone in that room the entire duration of my pregnancy.

Each of our older children has possession of their own bedroom, so when we decided on a room for the nursery, the only logical room was the little spare bedroom by our master bedroom. This particular room always experienced the most activity with a couple of psychics feeling that this room may have a 'porthole'. Although active, this room for the past several months felt calm and non-eventful.

We painted and redecorated the room into a beautiful nursery fit for any little princess. I bought a baby monitor complete with detection lights and an audible device for our new baby. Even though the room was next to ours, I didn't want to take any chances due to my uneasiness with this room.

On February 7th our beautiful baby daughter Sofia made her appearance into this world. Sofia was absolutely perfect. Upon arrival to her new home from the hospital I decided for our little blessing to occupy our room for a few weeks. Being a nurturing mother that I am, I just wasn't ready to for my baby Sofia to be in her own room.

Several nights later I decided that we would all sleep better if I placed our newborn in her nursery. I begin feeling that I may be a bit silly by not using the nursery that provided comfort and protection for my tiny Sofia. The nursery was right next to our bedroom, I had the baby monitor and the house and room had been uneventful and inactive for quite some time now.

On the third night of Sofia sleeping in her nursery I woke up to sounds on the baby monitor. Not only was there sounds emanating from the monitor, but the detection lights were flashing as well. I know without a doubt that it was not my imagination on what I heard through the monitor. It was a woman's voice in a low whisper and I couldn't make out what she was saying. I rationalized that maybe I was picking up another monitor on the same frequency in the neighborhood or something else that would make logical sense. Suddenly I heard the baby mobile from Sofia's crib start playing. The baby mobile is the type you manually wind and flip a button for it to come on. There were no other family members awake in the house at this time. I immediately jumped out of bed and ran into the nursery thinking maybe someone was in our house. What I found would frighten any parent. Sofia was about 2-3 weeks old when this incident happened, and she was unable to roll over or anything at this time. What I found when I got to her was astonishing. No one was in the room, but Sofia had been placed at the opposite end of the crib! She lay there gently sleeping with her blanket neatly covering her and her mobile was playing as if someone was tending to her. As I looked upon my baby, I realized that I had not awakened at my usual time to check on her. I have no explanation of how she was moved. No one in our home had got up with her and I could not explain the woman I heard over the baby monitor. From that night on I didn't let her sleep in that room again. She slept near me.

After looking back on this this experience years later, I believe someone may have been looking after both of us and realized just how tired I was.

Another experience that involved my new baby took place shortly after her birth as well. One of my loving and peaceful moments with my newborn is to hold and rock my baby. It would sooth her and she would quickly fall asleep. Many times I would hum a lullaby as I rocked her. Each time I would hum, I would hear someone in the distance mimicking my humming. At first I thought I may just be hearing the television from the other room or one of our other children humming too. This kept going on and I finally called Rick to come and investigate. He too felt there was someone in the nursery room, a woman who had come through that lost her baby and her life during child birth. She was here to experience motherhood and somehow ended up in my house. I think they knew Rick would always intervene and hear their story. Shortly after Rick's acknowledgement of her presence, she apparently left as I never heard or felt her again.

Rick's Thoughts

One of the many blessings in a mother's life is the birth of her newborn child. The bond created between mother and her baby; sharing one body, one breathe, one nutrients of nourishment, one love during pregnancy. The physical experience as the baby grows in the womb, cherishing each kick and heartbeat to validate presence of life. That ultimate moment when the mother hears the cry of announcement that her cherished blessing is upon the presence of earth. Of course the Father of the child receives special moments during this time as well – but different from what the mother receives. It is special like no other.

One of the many questions I receive is 'Rick, will a mother be with her child in the afterlife?" The moment the spirit is created and transcends into the physical body of their mother, the eternal bond is created. It will never change by any reason, even if the child's earthly path will never be taken in steps physically – such as a miscarriage.

Often I receive from moms who have experienced a short term pregnancy they always 'knew within' that their unborn baby was a boy or a girl. They cannot explain how they know – they just know. I believe the mother knows simply as their own spirit bonded with the spirit of the newborn.

It is another amazing part of life that even the most intelligent cannot fully explain, but the spiritual bond is valid.

So why was the mother in spirit in the nursery of K's newborn child? Was she attempting to build a fear so that K would no longer utilize the room as a nursery? Could there be any negative reasons such as the one in spirit felt the baby should be hers, or should I dare say – it was a reincarnation of her own child?

The answer is logical when you place into perspective of the spirit herself. She is a loving mother, spirit our otherwise. She knew the challenge K had endured being bedridden during pregnancy for those months. She knew the concerns that K felt bringing a new baby into an 'active' home that had experienced paranormal activity. Above all, the mother in spirit knew how much a baby is to be cherished and loved. The lady in spirit, is a mom.

She was assisting K and her new arrival. Protecting the baby while her mother was doing her very best to receive a few hours of sleep. Watching over the blessing in a blanket while Sofia slept, nurturing her, calming her, and doing what a mom does. I believe that the mother in spirit understood the love a baby brings into the home, as she too experienced the same.

I feel that as K's baby would grow and become more accustomed to her new surroundings, the presence of the mother in spirit would have become less prominent. She was with her baby now, as the bond of a mother and child are spiritually eternal.

You're Not Crazy You Have A Ghost

Bonus Chapter II

Knocks and Screams

Strange occurrences continue to happen and eventually the majority of my friends no longer thought I was crazy. A couple of my friends that lived close by actually requested that I give them a call if anything weird was to occur in my home. They wanted to see it for themselves.

One early morning I kept hearing the sounds of knocking on my attic door. There would be two knocks, a short pause, and another two knocks. This would continue on for quite some time. I decided to respond by knocking back on the door. Upon doing so and each time I responded with a knock, I would receive a return knock from the attic. After doing this several times with a response, I decided to call one of those friends who had requested I contact her if I have anything weird going on. Within minutes of calling her, my friend and her son arrived to my home to see it personally. I felt that she really did not believe me, and my thoughts were that she was there to see if it was truly happening or not.

My friend walked into my home and when I explained what was going on with the knocking, she paused for a moment and knocked on our entry door. As quickly as I had received a knocking response, she too received the same. She completely freaked out and ready to leave immediately.

On another occasion the same friend and her son came by for a neighborly visit. Her son was the same age as my son, and they had created a bond of friendship. The boys were playing outdoors while we were inside upstairs going through some of my clothes she wanted to borrow for an upcoming event. Suddenly we both heard the sound of a boy screaming in agony across the baby monitor. The lights were also reacting to the scream. We both run outside fearing one of our boys may have gotten hurt. When we got outside the boys were way in the back of the house throwing a football back and forth. No one was screaming anywhere in the area and neither of the boys had heard anything. To this day we do not know who or what was screaming in pain on the monitor.

The scream occurred once again on yet another evening. What I heard appeared to be the screaming of someone in agony. This time I thought maybe it was from the adjoining ball field and park in back of our house. It was a very dark night and I was afraid someone was being attacked or had got hurt at the park. I began walking towards the park to see if someone was hurt, but being alone I decided if someone was hurt or being hurt, I might be next one. I called 911 and reported what I heard. They sent an officer to investigate but didn't find anything or anyone to collaborate with the eerie screams.

One afternoon I thought I saw a woman's face appear in the nursery. I had feelings like I seen this woman practically each time I walked past the nursery. I called one of the neighbors who wanted immediately stated that she wanted to see for herself. She came right over and ran up the stairs into the room. A few moments later, with a pale complexion she turned to look at me and said "I see her!". She decided we weren't so crazy after all and quickly left to return home. She never requested to call her again if something odd was going on in my home.

Many strange occurrences take place in the neighborhood area this home resides. Many homes and businesses have documented strange experiences. During my research at the local library of my home I found documented cases of experiences that had been reported in this area since the 1800's. A woman was seen walking down the main street in period clothing for many years. Possibly a spiritual port hole was in this area or maybe something traumatic happened in the past. Personally I do not know the reason for the many reported incidents - but I do have my own personal thoughts.

Rick's Thoughts

Life is a continual process of learning, growing, experiencing, and evolving. Upon birth into the physical body, one is created to develop all the senses given. With the first breath, most babies learn the ability of feeling the touch of a human hand. The baby's physical body feels the warmth of a swaddling blanket and the sound of their voice with a cry. Within a short time, they hear the sounds of their environment and their tiny eyes embrace the sight of all around them. The birth of the spirit into the physical body is given the opportunity to embrace the amazing gifts of the five senses.

Through the years one or more of the five senses will be continually utilized along the physical path of earthly life. Some of us will actually enhance one of the five senses to compensate for lack of another. With each moment, we learn and grow with each touch, sound, sight, taste, and smell. One continues to do so to the completion of their time in the physical body and the return to the spirit body. It is the cycle of life continual.

In the body of spirit we no longer are in the vehicle of the physical body that includes the five senses, but that does not mean we no longer utilize nor experience what the five sense give. One in spirit understands the value of our senses, as they once experienced the life in the physical body as well. With that being said, of course they give us 'signs' to acknowledge their presence.

Since the writing of this book several years ago, I have received the opportunity to consult and visit with hundreds of thousands of individuals. I have also listened to hundreds of thousands who have shared their 'sign' validations from their loved ones in spirit. Physical signs that is common in the utilizing of our five senses yet unique in utilizing the 'sixth sense'.

The physical sign of sound. Hearing footsteps walking up a stairway, or a door shutting seemingly on its own. Setting in your favorite sofa and suddenly hearing someone whisper your name, and you are the only one in the room. The sound of feint music playing, yet there is not a radio or music device in sight. These are but a few of the many validations of a loved one in spirit utilizing their presence.

The physical sign of sight. Lounging in your den watching television and noticing a 'shadow figure' in the corner of your eye. You turned to look and no one is there. Visiting an historic location while on vacation and thought you saw a lady in period costume standing next to the door as if greeting those who entered. Waking up in the middle of the night by what appeared to be your grandmother setting at the foot of your bed, yet she had moved on years ago. Watching an object appear to move on its own, then return to its original position. These are but a few of the many validations of a loved one in spirit utilizing their presence.

The physical signs of feelings and smell. Walking into a room and feeling as if someone is there, but yet physically no one is in the room. Standing in a certain location in your home and suddenly having the feeling that someone has touched your arm or shoulder. Arriving at a friend's home and immediately feeling a sense of an emotion from something or someone whose presence is not in a physical form. Relaxing in your grandfather's favorite chair and smelling the aroma of his pipe tobacco. Having thoughts of your mother who has moved on and receiving the aroma of her perfume that she always wore. These are but a few of the many validations of a loved one is spirit utilizing their presence.

Our loved ones in spirit understand that we possess the five senses of our physical body, as they once also utilized these five senses while in the physical body. In knowing, loved ones in spirit will capture our attention with sound, sight, feelings, aroma, and even taste. It is not to create fear within us or to build a negative foundation. Loved ones in spirit are simply saying 'Hello, I am here. Can you see, feel, hear, and smell me?" If you think about it, would you not do the same to capture attention of another?

Bonus Chapter III

New Friendships

At one local book signing event an older woman with a great personality came up to me after the event and began talking to me. She stated how she really enjoyed the book, and had met Rick in the recent past for a personal reading. The lady explained she too had psychic abilities, and began telling me all sorts of things about me that she could not have known. She also spoke about her own paranormal experiences. I really enjoyed speaking with her and found her completely amazing and very interesting.

As she continued sharing her experiences, I felt that I could have listened to her all day. After a few pleasant moments of conversation, my new friend shared that she had a group of friends that all had abilities of some sort and they all got together from time to time and learn from each other. She invited me to attend the next event. I couldn't wait to meet everyone but wondered what kind of people I was going to meet. I really wanted to be able to meet more people like me that had paranormal experiences in their life. I also had never been able to openly talk to anyone except Rick about any of the things happened to me during my childhood. I had been made to feel evil about even talking about it. I wondered if they had the same things happen to them.

When I arrived at this get together I was amazed at how genuine and open everyone was to discuss spirituality and the paranormal. The age ranges of those attending at the party were from 20 something up to people in their 70's. I found that everyone was pleasantly relating to each other and not being judgmental of one another's thoughts. Everyone at the party was completely open to the other's abilities, with a willingness to listen and learn from one other. There were even those at this party who worked with government agencies to find missing people. I found everyone to be pleasant and genuine.

Everyone at this get together had similar stories that I had growing up during my childhood years and having to hide the things that were happening to them. Many were told they were evil or crazy. Not one of us asked to have this happen to us and all afraid to embrace it until we could no longer control or deny it. The greatest thing I found while talking with my new friends was that we all retained our abilities, and had utilized them in some way to help others in crisis.

To this day I still get with this group whenever I can and work hard at learning from each and every one who is making their spiritual abilities a part of life.

Rick's Thoughts

For many years before, during, and after the first publishing of this book I have shared the following: "We all are given many gifts upon creation, including the gift of knowing our loved ones in spirit are around us."

Society has labeled one's gifts as natural born talent, unique abilities, and even as a God given gift. A tremendous athlete appearing to naturally adapt to record achievements, without a break of sweat. An artist able to take a blank canvas and with a brush of color will create an original masterpiece like no other. An amazing chef that adds ingredients with ease and create a gourmet meal that can only be defined as a delectable delight. The individual with the uncanny ability to envision a future action or share a message from a loved one in spirit, and defined as psychic or medium. With every amazement shared upon creation, society has chosen to define these as only given to a chosen few.

As a child we begin to notice and accept the gifts given for life's purpose. A child who is attracted to crayons and drawing develops art along their life. A child who naturally adapts to the sound of music, and develops musical creations along their life. A child who that tends to share messages from loved ones no longer in the physical body, and develops psychic and mediumship abilities along their life. All began with a purpose, for a purpose along life.

As one grows into their adulthood, the ability to take ownership of what is given becomes an individual choice. With the abilities of what is defined as psychic and medium abilities, many resolved to block or ignore what is given. There are many reasons why. The religion of man that shares a traditional belief of what is right and what is wrong. The environment one resides or is employed, and may be outcast based on certain ideas and stipulations. I could name many more, for I too walked the path of life with psychic medium abilities and experienced the reasons why to block them. Fortunately I knew they were not to be shunned, and the right moment appeared for me to share what was given.

A gift is not ever to be dissolved but rather to be evolved. With confidence and a removal of fear one will manifest abundance in life's path – that is to be shared.

Bonus Chapter IV

Life After The Home

After the first edition of this book was published, many life events took place. The economy went belly up, and I filed for divorce. I was also one of those people unfortunately that had accepted a mortgage loan on the home that was one of those at the time was great for the broker but a financial burden on me. Being the only one working in our house on a regular basis and placed on bedrest during my pregnancy, things got out of control financially very fast. Everything in life was falling apart and I soon realized that I was not going to be able to keep up with this house on my own. I was going to have to make the sad decision to move. I begin searching for a new home and found one which would be more affordable and with less upkeep. Although I dearly loved my old dream home, I just could not maintain the house and all of its constant repairs. It was hard for me to come to this decision, but I had to do what I had to do. I spent many days crying over my decision. Although the weirdness in the home was consistently occurring, it had become more exciting than frightening. In some odd way the "regulars" had become almost like family and felt I would truly miss them.

The time had finally arrived for moving day. I felt I needed closure from all my experiences, so I called Rick and explained to him my mixed emotions about moving out. A part of me was relieved although I felt guilty feeling this emotion. I succumbed to the fact that life's events and the things happening all the time in the house were draining me. In reality, I found a home more cost effective and my stress levels I felt would actually improve. Rick agreed to come over on my last day in the house to help me with my closure. Just as everything seemed so "paranormal" on my first day in the house, my last day seemed quite "normal". I guess I wanted something else to happen just as an affirmation to my time there.

As Rick and I sat in the living room discussing my move, Rick relayed he felt like maybe this house could be mine again. I felt he was wrong. Sure enough, ten years later I had the opportunity to buy this home back. I really thought about it but decided not to repurchase it. Looking back on my time in this old house I know it was a path I needed to take. I was in need of an adventure and I had received it through this home. The process I went through with the renovation and the paranormal experiences changed me for the better. I got back some of my ambition for life, and my confidence level greatly improved. And most of all I met so many amazing people along my life's path.

My children still talk about the things that happened to them during this time in our life and how it has positively affected them. My son had all the experiences with the Civil War soldier during our years living in the home. Due to this experience, he became very interested in the military. My son joined the National Guard soon after high school. Our civil war ghost appeared to still be looking after him. While in the National Guard, my son was instructed that he was placed on standby to be deployed to Iraq. Of course we were all having anxiety over this announcement, but as most young soldiers he was ready and eager to go. He stated that the only thing he felt was there was going to be an accident and he would lose his legs. One night he said he woke up and seen "Garrison" by his bed. Garrison was very stern and told him "when you are in the building and the shooting starts go to the lowest level" and then he vanished. I am happy to write that the good news is his unit did not end up going to Iraq. My son said Garrison's words were very real and stern. If ever in that type of situation my son stated that he would head Garrison's words.

My oldest daughter never liked the paranormal stuff too much but learned to love the history of it. Due to the experiences of the home though, she is now teaching History in the St. Louis Missouri area. She looks at things very differently and feels while living in the home had received a history experience through the eyes of the ones actually there. She also is now the mother of my first grandchild Lillie. The first place she headed for to search for baby names was our family cemetery. Lillie Grace is named after her Great -Great -Great Grandmother. I think this was a way for my daughter to pay her respects to an amazing woman in our family that was way beyond her time. I don't believe things like this would have crossed her mind if it hadn't been for her time in our amazing home.

My youngest daughter was too young to remember anything she experienced in the home. However I quickly recognized her psychic abilities. She says she sees things all the time. Maybe our open minded thinking has made her more comfortable with her abilities and she will not out grow them.

The one thing about writing this book and acknowledging things I cannot explain did for me was the opportunity to meet many people like me. I met many who were going through the same incidents I was going through and expressed gratitude for sharing my story. I greatly enjoyed talking to each of them, and continue to meet many new friends. I feel writing this book has not only helped me in my life, but hopefully has given to others the realization that there are things that go on that we can't explain all over the world.

Rick's Thoughts

'You're Not Crazy You Have A Ghost" began with an idea while two friends were standing in a kitchen of a lovely Victorian home. The written words were to share experiences that would hopefully assist others in partnership to understand you are not alone. It was a book of reflections, experiences, thoughts, and friendship. The book was collaboration between two friends, to share with many new friends.

The opportunity and experiencing the activity of the home were moments of unforgettable reflections. Writing 'You're Not Crazy You Have A Ghost' were words printed never to be forgotten.

Years have pass since first setting down to write the first chapter, and many opportunities have manifested. Since the book, I have had the pleasure to meet thousands who have shared similar experiences within their home. I have had opportunities to assist others, and to observe how they too began the process of knowing the presence of activity is a validation to understand. My co-author and I lives have since individually changed as life should, with new opportunities and blessings. I have observed my friend and co-author's family grow, her young children who once accepted what is while living within the home to adults paving a life of abundance. In my observation, the home's activity became a stepping stone for my co-author and her family, and a stronger family bond.

   I too feel there was a valid reason why this lovely Victorian home in a small town became a part of my life. The home was a confidence builder for the abilities I was given, and to understand these abilities would be the foundation of my purpose in life. The loved ones in spirit had a sense of pride for the home, as I too shall retain a sense of pride for my abilities. The home reflected that in life there will be times one will not fully understand the mysteries and uncertainties, but for every moment there is a reason for the experience. The old home of grandeur shared not to allow fear to hold you from what you are to be given in life, as I too have learned not to be afraid of sharing my abilities to the world. Built with lumber, nails, and pride, the home will be a memory that life is continual.

BElieve.

"You're Not Crazy, You Have A Ghost"

Photo Album From My Home

Photograph 1
The main stairway of my home where many experiences occur, including our visitor walking up and down the stairway. We captured this visitor walking up the stairway after hearing a strange sound. Notice the "pair of misty boots" on the top step.

Photograph 2
A photo of the main stairway taken just a few seconds before the photo above. Along the step where one would turn the corner, droplets of a "bloodlike" substance continues to appear to this day. Although we clean the area where the droplets appear, they continue to appear in an eerie fashion.

Photograph 3
Our main dining room. Many experiences occur in this room in which a few have been described within this book. Notice the clock on the wall. The clock has a tendency to "stop by an unseen hand" at approximately 1:27. This room is
also where our visitor assisted us with our decision whether to "paint or wallpaper".

Photograph 4
Another photo of our dining room. Many times we have entered this room to "view a visitor" standing in the corner.

Photograph 5
The "science project" that became a physical validation from the home's original owner. The first of two photographs. Notice within the steam the "beginning" shape of a face that is located in the center of the mist.

Photograph 6
The second photo of the science project taken a few seconds after the first photo above. The original owner made his presence known within the steam. The picture was validated by an old photo of the original owner, and his relative.

About The Authors

Rick Hayes is an author and the founder and creator of LifesGift, an association that supports Rick's psychic medium abilities. With the LifesGift website www.lifesgift.com, Rick consults regularly with those that have questions regarding life after death and one's daily path on earth. Rick's second book is called "Stepping Stones: Thoughts Along Life's Path."

At an early age, Rick realized that he had been given the unique ability to relay messages from those who have passed. Born and raised in a Christian environment, he continually struggled with his apparent gifts due to his upbringing. Although he would assist a select few with their grief of an apparent loss of a loved one, it wasn't until early 2002 that he decided to bring his ability to the public. A dear friend was going through the emotion of a loved one's near passing due to cancer. With Rick's assistance, the pain turned to comfort in knowing that life is everlasting. Her words changed Rick's life path. "You are being truly selfish by not sharing your gift with others" From that point on, Rick decided to follow his path that was apparently meant to be.

In May 2003, the LifesGift website was launched to assist in reaching those with questions in regards to life everlasting. Born in the Midwest, Rick resides in a small community near where he grew up as a child. He attended college in Florida with an extensive background in Marketing. Rick has three children, or as he calls "his best friends", and spends his spare moments sharing quality time with his family.

To contact Rick, email to rick@lifesgift.com

About The Authors

A Loving mother of seven children (including four step-children), K Coons resides in a beautiful rural setting in the Midwest. Because of K Coons's passion for decorating and home restoration, this lead her to the purchase of the home which is the subject of this book. K Coons grew up in a Christian background and because of her beliefs, struggled with the experiences that occurred in her new home. She felt a need to write this book, as to assist others that have or had similar occurrences.

To contact K Coons, email to rick@lifesgift.com

Other Books By Rick Hayes

Paperback and Kindle Amazon
Stepping Stones: Thoughts Along Life's Path
Stellium Books

You're Not Crazy You Have A Ghost

Also From Stellium Books
Best Seller Supernatural and Unexplained Mysteries
Amazon Top Ten

Amazing Paranormal Encounters

www.ingramcontent.com/pod-product-compliance
Lightning Source LLC
Chambersburg PA
CBHW060133100426
42744CB00007B/771